DAVID BOWIE

STORIES BEHIND THE SONGS 1970-1980

CHRIS WELCH

CARLTON
BOOKS

THIS IS A CARLTON BOOK

This edition published by Carlton Books Limited
20 Mortimer Street
London W1T 3JW

Text copyright © 1999, 2010 Chris Welch
Design copyright © 2010 Carlton Books Limited

A CIP catalogue for this book is available from the British Library

ISBN 978-1-84732-663-8

Printed and bound in China

The publishers would like to thank the following sources for their kind permission to reproduce the pictures in this book.

Corbis: /Lynn Goldsmith: 128; /Hulton Deutsch Collection: 136, 160; /Dennis O'Regan: 153, 169; / Neal Preston: 125
Getty Images: 117; /Fox Photos: 150
Kobal Collection: 123; /Rolf Thiele/MGM, Leguan: 144
London Features International: 10, 71, 81, 102, 141, 155, 184; /Imperial Press: 127; /Ilpo Musto: 69
Mary Evans Picture Library: 35
Mirrorpix: 22
Pictorial Press Ltd: 18, 26, 28, 37, 46, 48, 79, 113, 182-183; /Jeffrey Mayer: 12; /Peter Mazel: 59; /J. Stevens: 85; /Van Houten: 3t
Retna: /Jak Kilby: 189; /Michael Putland: 50
Rex Features: 3b, 53, 64, 67, 86, 192; /Chris Foster: 33; /Harry Goodwin: 191; /Fraser Gray: 118; / Dezo Hoffman: 14, 40; /Ray Stevenson: 19
©Mick Rock: 24, 56, 60, 89, 98
Richard I. Ward: 4, 6

Every effort has been made to acknowledge correctly and contact the source and/or copyright holder of each picture and Carlton Books Limited apologises for any unintentional errors or omissions that will be corrected in future editions of this book.

CONTENTS

THE EARLY RELEASES

Few artists have embraced so many changes of style, character and musical direction as David Bowie.

Yet throughout an extraordinary career that has spanned five decades, Bowie has retained the essential ingredients that have made him a legend. Magnetism, mystery, and conflicting strands of strength and vulnerability are characteristic of this enduringly popular figure and hugely influential artist.

Change has indeed been his life blood since Bowie first began his career as a performing artist. From 'Major Tom' to 'Ziggy Stardust' and from 'The Man Who Fell To Earth' to 'Thin White Duke', trend-setting Bowie has been changing not just himself but the world about him.

David Bowie has come a long way since he was the good-looking, young Mod vainly trying to break into the Sixties pop scene. In those pre-Ziggy days he was a penniless star waiting to be born, but then came the first of many changes, sparked as much by his restless, active mind as by the need for com-mercial success. The solo singer scored a resounding hit with 'Space Oddity' in 1969 but he was not satis-fied. Soon he embraced the vibrant new underground rock sounds that emanated from New York. Under the influence of Lou Reed and Iggy Pop, and aided by guitarist Mick Ronson, he created such astonishingly innova-tive albums as *The Man Who Sold The World, The Rise And Fall Of Ziggy Stardust And The Spiders From Mars,* and *Aladdin Sane*. They proved a sensation and amid the furore of controversy about his glit-tering pop image and overt sexuality, Bowie became the first androgynous rock star and, inadvertently, sparked the Glam Rock boom.

The early Seventies were golden years for Bowie and success did not stop coming even when he deliberately killed off Ziggy Stardust at a dramatic farewell concert in July, 1973. Bowie underwent more drastic changes in the years ahead, and was still undergoing this process of evolution in 1997, when he was 50. Although he sometimes strained the patience and loyalty of fans and critics, he invariably came up with songs, music, films, videos, concerts and albums that were always challenging and at the cutting edge. He has been full of surprises too. Only David, in the middle of Ziggy madness, could bring out

DAVID JONES IN
A CLASS PHOTO
TAKEN AT BROMLEY
TECHNICAL SCHOOL,
MAY 1959.

5

Pin Ups – an album of R & B covers. He delved into Germanic electro rock during his *Low* and *Heroes* period, and amid squeals of outrage from his oldest fans, formed a controversial neo-metal band appropriately called Tin Machine. He aroused the critics' wrath on many occasions by such perceived inconsistency. Apparently contradicting his proclaimed beliefs, Bowie undermined the faith of his supporters by shamelessly switching views on everything from sex to politics to his own background and influences. Indeed his life has been full of ironies.

As a Zen Buddhist he sought peace and humility, but also briefly flirted with ideas of supermen and fascism. A bisexual, he once proclaimed to the press that he was gay and then later admitted that he had said such things largely in the interests of publicity and promotion. And the idealistic youth, who once accused hippies of being capitalists, has become one of the richest men on the planet, worth countless millions, from astute business practices.

It's no wonder that some of his followers have sometimes felt let down. As a consequence, Bowie has been the victim of the most virulent and intense criticism. On one occasion, an enraged music critic virtually shouted at him "Sit down sir!" in an article that, apparently, had the victim in fits of unrestrained laughter.

Even members of his own family have been known to pile insults and abuse on his head. It is a measure of his almost hypnotic appeal that he can arouse

DAVID PLAYING SAX AND GUITAR WITH THE KON-RADS AT HILLSIDERS YOUTH CLUB, BIGGINS HILL, IN MAY 1963

such passions, ranging from idolatry to scorn. If he wasn't so special, nobody would care. Bowie has been called many things cold, manipulative, uncaring and even cynical. What critics fail to see is the restless, sensitive spirit who needs to seek all life's opportunities and attractions in order to find fulfilment and satisfaction. His need to move on has been paramount, even if the process has sometimes been hurtful. Having been brought up in suburbia, with its fixed ideas, fixed locations and stolid class values, Bowie desperately needed to escape to allow his imagination free rein. He had to explore, to find new friends, mentors and gurus, to experiment and embrace everything from ballet, mime and art to religion and modern jazz. Each new passion was seized upon with the boundless energy and enthusiasm of youth. Mod culture, hippie idealism, pop stardom and the politics of the record business were all a part of his life-forming experiences. In contrast with this image of Bowie the *avant garde*, hustling go-getter, there is another picture of Bowie as the exhausted flower child–lazy, petulant, tearful and unwilling to work. This is Bowie the bane of managers and record producers, the Bowie who preferred to stay idly in bed rather than get up and face the world.

However, the David Bowie that the pop community first encountered in the Sixties wasn't cold, idle or uncaring. Quite the reverse. He was, and remains, an essentially sensitive, considerate, hardworking, intelligent and charming person. In those early days he often seemed lonely and neglected, a far cry from the boisterous, swaggering image of Ziggy Stardust, the universal centre of attention. Young Bowie would give freely of his time, affections and commitment to people. This only made it all the more painful when he had to move on, in his ceaseless quest to make a more meaningful life for himself.

Bowie's changes affected family and friends as well as business and musical partners. He would form, quit and then break up bands. He changed managers, record labels, producers and musicians. He married and then divorced. He was a socialite and then a recluse; a globe-trotter and then an exile. He'd be promiscuous and experiment with drugs and then he'd reappear as an abstemious control freak. The red-haired rebel became a smart-suited, neatly-coiffeured business tycoon. The man who sold the world would duet with Bing Crosby on 'Little Drummer Boy'. The David Bowie who could produce 'The Laughing Gnome' also produced such uncompromising material as 'Hearts Filthy Lesson' from his 1995 album *Outside*.

Where did all this talent and this strange mixture of ideas and influences come from? David Robert Jones was born at Stansfield Road, Brixton, London on January 8, 1947.

His father was Haywood Stenton Jones (born 1912), and his mother was

Peggy Burns; she already had a son, Terry. The couple were married in September, 1947. In the mid-Fifties the family moved to Plaistow Grove, Bromley and Bowie went to Burnt Ash Junior School, and then Bromley Technical High School in 1958 where he met future Herd and Humble Pie guitarist Peter Frampton, whose father was a tutor at the school.

Bowie's early interest in jazz, poetry and beatnik culture was encouraged by his older half-brother Terry Burns, but Bowie also shared an interest in R & B with his school friend George Underwood. It was during a skirmish with Underwood, over a girlfriend, that Bowie sustained an eye injury that resulted in him having different coloured pupils, an attribute that has always made him appear somewhat other-worldly. Nevertheless, he and Underwood remained pals and together they formed Bowie's first pop group, The Kon-Rads, in July, 1962. Bowie sang and played saxophone with The Kon-Rads with Neville Wills and Alan Dodds (guitars), and Dave Cook (drums).

They tried and failed to get a Decca recording contract. Bowie now says that he quit the Kon-Rads in 1963 because they didn't want to play R & B and refused to play one of his favourite tunes 'Can I Get A Witness', preferring to play hits from the repertoire of Cliff Richard and The Shadows instead.

When Bowie left school in July, 1963 he began working as an assistant in an advertising agency. At the same time he continued to play the saxophone and began singing with local Bromley group The King Bees. With "David Jones" on vocals (sometimes Davie or Davy) the group included George Underwood, Bob Allen (drums), Dave Howard (bass) and Roger Bluck (guitar). The first sign of Bowie's determination to succeed came when he cheekily wrote to a business tycoon, the washing machine millionaire John Bloom, asking for assistance with his group. Bloom was sufficiently amused to pass on the request to Les Conn, an experienced music business agent who actually took on the fledgling band's management. As a result of his efforts, on June 5, 1964 David Jones and The King Bees were signed to Vocalion, a subsidiary of Decca, and released their first single 'Liza Jane' coupled with 'Louie Louie Go Home' a cover of a Paul Revere and The Raiders American hit.

In September, 1964 The King Bees released a second single 'You're Holding Me Down'/'I've Gotta' (Coral). It was a flop, the group split and Davy Jones joined an R & B group from Maidstone, Kent called The Manish Boys. A more professional band, they signed to Parlophone and in December, 1964 secured a tour with Gene Pitney, The Kinks and Marianne Faithfull.

On March 5, 1965, David Jones and The Manish Boys released 'I Pity The Fool'/'Take My Tip' (Parlophone) produced by Shel Talmy. 'Take My Tip' was Bowie's first original song on record and to boost the sound, top session man

Jimmy Page played lead guitar. Sadly none of these records were hits despite the best attempts at promotion, and The Manish Boys broke up. On August 20, 1965, Davy Jones released 'You've Got A Habit Of Leaving'/'Baby Loves That Way' (Parlophone) produced by Shel Talmy and backed by a new outfit called The Lower Third with Denis Taylor (guitar), Graham Rivens (bass) and Les Mighall (drums). The group was strongly influenced by The Who and even played support on Who gigs.

It was around this time that Bowie met pop manager Ken Pitt, who handled such bands as Manfred Mann and the Mark Leeman Five. Bowie was then being handled by Ralph Horton, an ex-Moody Blues roadie. Ken Pitt took over from Horton, signed Bowie for management and began the long process of grooming him for stardom. One of his first acts was to take Bowie away from Parlophone and get him signed to Pye. Few artists have been signed to quite so many different labels. The next decision would have more immediate personal impact. In January, 1966 Davie Jones changed his name to David Bowie to avoid confusion with Davy Jones of The Monkees. The name change was on the advice of Ken Pitt, who had heard all about the imminent launch of The Monkees in America and guessed that they would be mega successful. It was David who came up with the name Bowie (pronounced "Bo-wee" in honour of Jim Bowie, of hunting knife fame, and not as in Bow Wow). Bowie's own career was still on a knife edge as he consistently failed to make the charts, even with releases like 'Can't Help Thinking About Me'/'And I Say To Myself (Pye) credited to David Bowie although he was backed by The Lower Third. 'Can't Help Thinking About Me' has been hailed as one of the finest of his pre-1969 waxings and it actually got into the *Melody Maker* Top Forty. This epic, produced by Tony Hatch, was released in January, 1966. It was the first time the Bowie name was used and legend has it that when visiting Ken Pitt's London apartment the singer casually told his manager: "Oh by the way, I'm David Bowie now," to which Mr. Pitt replied "That's nice."

With a professional manager and the assistance of a top producer, it might have seemed that Bowie had a better chance of reaching the charts. During 1966 two more singles were unveiled including 'Do Anything You Say'/'Good Morning Girl' (Pye) and 'I Dig Everything'/'I'm Not Losing Sleep' (Pye). On the B side of the latter David sang in very English fashion "I feed the lions in Trafalgar Square and I dig everything." It was another flop. His contract with Pye ended in September and the Lower Third had been quietly left behind, replaced by a largely uncredited, short-lived backing group called The Buzz. Neither solo records had any luck. Bowie began working more as a solo performer combining the roles of a Dylan-esque folk singer with that of an

"OH BY THE WAY, I'M DAVID BOWIE NOW."

all-round entertainer. He had a small part in a film, appeared on TV and worked as a model. He starred in a short experimental film called *The Image* and his social life blossomed as he began going out with a dancer called Hermione Farthingale.

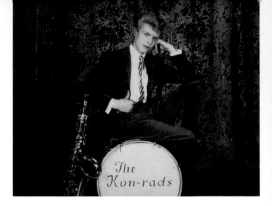

The Buzz comprised John Hutchinson (guitar), Dek Fearnley (bass), Derek Boyles (organ) and John Eager (drums). Bowie gigged with them at London's famed Marquee club before they broke up in July. At first Bowie accepted all the advice he could get – Pitt saw him appealing to a wider audience and was later castigated as the man who wanted David Bowie to be "the new Tommy Steele" and a kind of family entertainer. In fact it was Pitt who paved the way for his later association with the underground scene by introducing him to the Velvet Underground. In November, 1966, Ken Pitt visited New York on business and met such luminaries as Andy Warhol and Lou Reed, whom he hoped to represent in the UK as their agent. On his return to London he brought Bowie back a Velvet Underground album. It had far-reaching effects.

WHO COULD TURN DOWN THIS STAR OF THE FUTURE? ONLY DECCA RECORDS.

In the meantime Bowie was still being promoted as a very English singer/ songwriter, which was no bad thing as he was at last beginning to attract media attention and favourable reviews for his work. As the first R & B phase drew to a close, Bowie began to write songs that reflected his circumstances and surroundings. He was the eagle-eyed, sympathetic, witty observer of people and their foibles, and a keen student of the Mod culture that was part of the Soho scene. Many of his songs had a kind of music hall flavour, a characteristic he shared with fellow writers Steve Marriott, Pete Townshend and Ray Davies, although he tended to be more flowery and whimsical.

At the end of a bad business patch, manager Pitt secured a new record deal for Bowie, switching him from Pye to Decca. His next recordings appeared on Decca's independent arm, Deram, set up by top producer Denny Cordell. One of the first British indie labels, it boasted among its roster of acts Cat Stevens, who became Deram's most successful artist, shooting to stardom with 'I Love My Dog' and 'Matthew And Son.' Bowie didn't enjoy that kind of chart success for some time, but the new deal allowed him to make his first solo album *David Bowie*, released with high hopes on June 1, 1967. It was the first album released by a British artist who had not had a hit single. But that wasn't for want of trying. As a taster Deram released the single 'Rubber Band' coupled with another song 'The London Boys' (December, 1966). 'Rubber

Band' was also released in the US with 'There Is A Happy Land' on the B side, also from the LP. 'The London Boys', a particularly fine per-formance, was later included on a Decca repackaged version of the album called *The World Of David Bowie* (1970).

'Rubber Band,' 'The London Boys,' and 'Please Mr Gravedigger' had first been recorded as demos at RG Jones Studios in Surrey, a studio often used by The Yardbirds. 'Rubber Band' was not the best choice for a first single. Although The Beatles, with their varied and increasingly experimental output, had proved you could use strings, brass and any other kind of backing on a pop record and still sound hip, here it didn't quite work and the public remained unmoved. Even so it remains an attractive, inventive composition by the 19-year-old, with the lyrics displaying a gentle, subtle humour. The scene is 1914 and the Rubber Band are playing "tunes out of tune" in the library gardens (doubtless the long-established Library Gardens in Bromley near to where Bowie worked). The conductor waves his little golden wand and presides over a moustache "stiffly waxed and one foot long". The performance becomes ever more lugubrious until Bowie deftly introduces a manic note, shouting "Oh play that thing!" off mike during a trumpet solo. He is also heard muttering "I hope you break your baton" in the denouement, when it is finally revealed that, during the war, the dastardly conductor has gone off with the composer's girl.

It's like a Victorian music hall item and Bowie delivers it with charming, theatrical sophistication.

His next single, released on April 14, 1967, was 'The Laughing Gnome'/'The Gospel According To Tony Day'. The Gnome Song has been the subject of hot debate among Bowie aficionados for years. Made under the auspices of producer Mike Vernon, it has some speeded up Chipmunks-style effects and lots of jokes. Bowie cheerfully tells the tale of the gnome that he puts on a train to the seaside only to find him sitting at the end of his bed in the morning. The speeded-up voice of the laughing gnome is actually engineer Gus Dudgeon, who later went on to work with Elton John and The Bonzo Dog Doo Dah Band. He helped Bowie come up with many of the gags used on the record. Most thought it very funny, enjoyed all the dreadful puns and realized Bowie was enjoying himself down among the session men.

However, many did not see the joke. *Melody Maker* writer Michael Watts, who later did so much to promote Bowie's career during his Ziggy Stardust era, looked utterly scornful and curled his lip whenever anyone dared mention the dreaded Gnome Song. There is definitely a split between Bowie fans of the first and second epochs. A lot of commentators actually preferred the Deram period Bowie to the RCA superstar poseur, and many hardcore Bowie fans agreed.

Years later they would shout out for 'The Laughing Gnome' at Tin Machine concerts – Bowie would pretend not to hear these requests. In a final irony, after Bowie had desperately tried to get a hit throughout the early Sixties, when 'The Laughing Gnome' was re-issued on September 8, 1973 it rocketed to Number 4 in the UK charts. "Haven't you got a gnome to go to?"

Guitarist Davy O'List of The Nice was one of the first rock musicians to turn on to the rising young singer's work. He bought a copy of *The World of David Bowie* when it hit the shops and played it to anyone who would listen. Davy and The Nice enthused about the songs and, in particular, the singer's voice with its unusual range and ability to span a variety of moods and emotions. Clearly David Bowie was becoming a much-respected name among the cognoscenti. The Nice listened constantly to the Deram album and were intrigued by the lyrics and the hidden subtleties and in-jokes that particularly appealed to musicians. The clarity of Bowie's diction and the English accent were regarded as refreshingly different.

STRUMMING A NEAT GUITAR, BOWIE GOES FOLK.

Produced by Mike Vernon, Bowie's first album tracks included 'Uncle Arthur', 'Sell Me A Coat', 'Rubber Band', 'Love You Till Tuesday', 'There Is A Happy Land', 'We Are Hungry Men', 'When I Live My Dream', 'Little Bombardier', 'Silly Boy Blue', 'Come And Buy My Toys', 'Join The Gang', 'She's Got Medals', 'Maids Of Bond Street' and 'Please Mr Gravedigger.'

Each of the songs had its own character and overall the album has the flavour of a Lionel Bart musical as sung by Anthony Newley. (Coincidentally both Bart and Newley died in April, 1999.) Says Bowie: "I did a lot of Newley things on the very first album I made. I was the world's worst mimic. I WAS Anthony Newley for a year. He was one of the most talented men England ever produced."

Indeed Newley was unusual among post-War British artists in being able to bestride the worlds of both show business and pop music. He also introduced an authentic working class voice into popular culture. As a child star he played The Artful Dodger in the 1948 movie version of *Oliver Twist*. He became an overnight pop star when he sang rock 'n' roll in the movie *Idle On Parade* and went on to enjoy distinctive Number 1 hits with 'Why' and 'Do You Mind'. More hits followed with the comic 'Strawberry Fair' and heroic 'What Kind Of Fool Am I?' However, what impressed Bowie most was Newley's off-beat TV show *The World Of Gurney Slade*, a long-forgotten precursor of *Monty*

Python's Flying Circus. Newley, first married to Joan Collins, also wrote and starred in the West End musicals *Stop The World I Want To Get Off* and *The Roar Of The Greasepaint – the Smell Of The Crowd*.

Newley later moved to America, where he spent most of his subsequent career, although he returned home to play a part in BBC TV's popular series *East Enders*. He died from cancer at his home in Florida on April 14, 1999, aged 67.

Despite Bowie's respect for Newley, it is said that when a music publisher sent the latter a copy of Bowie's 1967 album he smashed the record in high dudgeon. Bowie didn't resort to blatant Newley-isms on every song. He merely utilized the drawl shared by many residents of the South London suburbs. It is particularly noticeable on 'London Boys', a heavily-arranged orchestral number built around Bowie's account of a Mod boy's adventures on Wardour Street, where he wanders far away from home, taking lots of pills and feeling very ill.

Other songs are quite knowing, debating topics that the average teenage innocent in the Sixties would have known little or nothing about. 'She's Got Medals' tells of a woman who becomes a man and joins the army. She wears hobnailed boots, plays darts and stands her round of drinks. Later 'he' returns to London to resume her role as a woman. 'She's Got Medals' is full of double entendres.

There are many other examples of sophisticated, unpredictable ideas, like the apocalyptic 'Please Mr Gravedigger' with its tale of bombs raining down on a cemetery. But the song that caught most people's attention and seemed the most likely to succeed was 'Love You Till Tuesday', a charming evocation of the short lived nature of love. It was probably very appropriate for Bowie at a time when he was constantly pursued by suitors and experienced a range of affairs. *A Melody Maker* review of the single, in July, 1967, stated: "David Bowie is one of the few really original solo singers operating in the theatre of British pop. He writes very unusual material, he's good-looking and while his voice has Anthony Newley connotations it matters little while he makes fine records of this ilk." The song was described as being "very funny" and as deserving of "instant recognition".

Ken Pitt put up £7,000 to make a promo film of the song, but Deram dropped Bowie, which meant he had now been with five labels. To rub salt into the wounds, the label had turned down the last three singles that Bowie and his manager offered including 'Let Me Sleep Beside You', 'When I Live My Dream', and 'In The Heat Of The Morning' coupled with 'London Bye Ta Ta'. No wonder Bowie almost gave up the pop scene. He took a greater interest in ballet, theatre and Buddhism and he became heavily involved with Lindsay

> *"I **WAS** ANTHONY NEWLEY FOR A YEAR. HE WAS ONE OF THE MOST TALENTED MEN ENGLAND EVER PRODUCED."*
>
> DAVID BOWIE

13

Kemp, the famous mime artist. Bowie made his mime debut with Kemp in *Pierrot In Turquoise* at the New Theatre, Oxford on December 28, 1967. He even went off to a Buddhist monastery in Scotland for a while. When he returned to London the hippie scene was taking off and he opened his own Arts Lab at the Three Tuns, Beckenham, where he was the star attraction.

Together with girlfriend, Hermione Farthingale, and John Hutchinson he formed his own mime troupe called Feathers, but this broke up when Hermione and Bowie split up while he was away filming. Just when it seemed he might be doomed to wander forever in a kind of theatrical wilderness, a song that he had written while filming 'Love You Till Tuesday' held out the promise of pop success. The new one had a strangely haunting theme, which instantly captivated the technicians working on the film set – they began humming the melody. The song was about an astronaut called Major Tom who was marooned in space above the blue planet Earth, and was feeling "rather strange". Bowie had recently been inspired by a visit to the cinema to see the late Stanley Kubrick's astonishing cinematic masterpiece *2001: A Space Odyssey*.

Says Bowie: "A number of films made a deep impression on me in the Sixties and one of the most important was Stanley Kubrick's 2001. I related to the sense of isolation. That and a number of other elements set the pattern for a lot of the kinds of music that I wrote and the kinds of performances that I gave, and probably predicted my lifestyle for the Seventies."

When Bowie sang "Ground control to Major Tom" in those sombre tones, it captured the mood of the moment and became one of the most famous and most frequently quoted opening lines to a pop song. Real-life American astronauts were about to make their first landing on the Moon, and the tapped into the public consciousness.

Even then it wasn't an instant rocket ride to the top; there were problems to overcome. One of these was that producer Tony Visconti did not want to have anything to do with the song that went on to become Bowie's first hit and a pop classic. In the end it was left to engineer Gus Dudgeon to work on the song that Bowie called 'Space Oddity'. When Ken Pitt took the film clip along to Mercury to show them Bowie acting the part of Major Tom, Mercury liked the idea sufficiently to sign Bowie in June, 1969, and recording sessions began right away.

Gus Dudgeon had known Bowie from his work with Mike Vernon at Deram and appreciated his originality and sense of humour: "We had a lot of fun together and yes, I'm afraid I am a laughing gnome!" He has no idea why Tony Visconti did not like the idea of 'Space Oddity' but the feeling was that Bowie was somehow compromising his art by daring to be topical in the search for a hit. Dudgeon insists that the idea was to make a typically David Bowie record: "When I listened to the demo of 'Major Tom' I thought it was incredible. I couldn't believe that Tony didn't want to do it." After discussions, Visconti told Dudgeon to do the single and he would do the album himself.

Musicians on the 'Space Oddity' session were Mick Wayne (guitar), Rick Wakeman (Mellotron), Herbie Flowers (bass) and Terry Cox (drums). Dudgeon recalls a spotty young Wakeman turning up late for the session, explaining that he had been stuck on a Tube train getting to the studio. However the Mellotron, a unique keyboard instrument that relied on revolving tape loops to create an eerie orchestral sound, was a great asset to the production. It was one of Wakeman's earliest sessions and he got the parts down in two takes.

Adding to the unique spacey sound was Bowie's Stylophone, a simple instrument played with a pen or stylus. (At the time the Stylophone was a recent invention that was also very popular with Rolf Harris.) Gus Dudgeon sketched out some ideas for a string arrangement and Paul Buck master put them together in a playable form for the musicians. To take advantage of this array of unusual instruments and ideas the single was one of the first to be released in stereophonic sound.

'Space Oddity' was played for the first time at the Rolling Stones' Free Concert in Hyde Park that summer and it was released on the Philips label (the company having taken over Mercury) on July 11, 1969, with 'Wild Eyed Boy From Freecloud' on the B side. At the same time Bowie began recording his first album for the label, with Tony Visconti.

On July 20, 1969 Neil Armstrong disembarked from his 'tin can' and landed on the Moon. People the world over were glued to their television sets watching the events as they happened, while anyone turning on their radio stood a good chance of hearing David Bowie singing 'Space Oddity'. Yet the record still only managed to creep up to Number 48 in the UK charts and made no impression at all in the US. After a week in the charts the record was actually withdrawn and it looked as if Philips had lost all faith in its new signing. And then a miracle happened – DJs took up the record and continued to give it airtime, 'Space Oddity' was reissued, and this time it shot up the UK charts to peak at Number 5. It stayed in the charts for 13 weeks and at last David Bowie was a pop star, much in demand for press interviews and TV appearances.

Oddly enough, the single was one of a trilogy of hits produced by Gus Dudgeon that had connections with space. 'I'm The Urban Spaceman' had been a Number 5 hit for The Bonzo Dog Doo Dah Band in 1968, Bowie's 'Space Oddity' came the following year and Elton John's 'Rocket Man' got to Number 2 in 1972.

It had been a long haul from the King Bees and 'Liza Jane', Bowie's debut single in 1964, but 'Space Oddity' was only the start – the real drama and excitement lay ahead. The record returned to haunt him when it was reissued on RCA in October, 1975, and gave Bowie his first British Number 1. It was also a hit in the US when it got to Number 15 in the *Billboard* chart in February, 1973. So while Bowie was, musically speaking, light years ahead, and even while he was in the throes of promoting such albums as *Aladdin Sane*, his past was constantly coming back to haunt him.

In the aftermath of 'Space Oddity' Bowie had to cope with being the object of teenage affection and fan hysteria – he found being screamed at a strange experience that left him somewhat dazed and confused. Earlier in the year he had met a feisty young American visitor to London, Angela Barnett. She had already seen him perform and they finally met up at the Speakeasy Club in Margaret Street, during a press party for the latest King Crimson album.

The pair quickly became an item and lived together in Beckenham, where they ran the Arts Lab in response to the nationwide hippie movement, trying to encourage young people to be creative. It was a good idea but Bowie gave up on the Arts Lab concept when he realized that most people were coming just to see him perform and not to participate. However he helped organize a Free Festival in Beckenham Park held on August 11, 1969. It took place only a few days after the funeral of his father Haywood Stenton Jones, who died of pneumonia on August 5. Bowie had heard the news of his father's death while recording his album with Tony Visconti at Trident Studios.

By the end of the year Bowie returned to "live" work and in October he began a tour with Humble Pie and Love Sculpture. During his solo acoustic set he attempted to play 'Space Oddity', which was apparently greeted with jeers and boos by skinhead rock fans. This came both as a great shock and as a disappointment to the sensitive young singer still coping with his personal grief and sense of loss. However, the hostile reaction to some of his shows on the Humble Pie tour had a positive effect, encouraging Bowie, sub-consciously, to bury himself inside a protective stage persona. The idea of Ziggy Stardust took root.

His second album *David Bowie* (Philips) was completed and released on November 4, 1969. It was issued in the US under the title *Man Of Words, Man Of Music* (Mercury) and re-released in the UK as *Space Oddity* by RCA in October, 1972.

The tracks included 'Space Oddity', 'Unwashed And Somewhat Slightly Dazed', 'Letter To Hermione', 'Cygnet Committee', 'Janine', 'An Occasional Dream', 'Wild Eyed Boy From Freecloud', 'God Knows I'm Good', and 'Memory Of A Free Festival'.

Produced by Tony Visconti and Gus Dudgeon, the backing musicians were Tony Visconti (bass), Rick Wakeman (keyboards) and Terry Cox and John Cambridge (drums). Further assistance came from Paul Buckmaster, Keith Christmas, Mick Wayne, Tim Renwick, Herbie Flowers and Benny Marshall.

The album version of 'Space Oddity' was much longer than the single. Few today would dare make a record aimed at the chart, opening with desultory acoustic guitar chords and military snare drum rat-a-tats. Yet this is how Bowie's masterpiece is gently ushered in. The space pilot, Major Tom, is advised by Ground Control to take his protein pills and put his helmet on. As the countdown for lift-off into outer space begins, we hear Bowie's double-tracked voice singing a duet with himself as Wakeman's Mellotron accompanies the Major into orbit and Tom reports back to Earth that "the stars look very different today". He sits in his tin can and notes that "Planet Earth is blue and there's nothing I can do". Eventually his circuits go dead and he is left helpless in space, sending messages of love to his wife. His dilemma is exacerbated by the sound of the string section de-tuning for the final bars. It's a conceptual gem and, as such, sits uneasily with the rest of the material, which is quite different.

DAVID BOWIE
PLAYS *Stylophone*
ON 'SPACE ODDITY'

'PLAY ALONG WITH THE GROUPS'

The greatest CRAZE since the YO-YO . . . the fantastic STYLOPHONE used by DAVID BOWIE in 'SPACE ODDITY' has created this new and wonderfully exciting craze. This is how it works.
The STYLOPHONE is a pocket electronic organ with a completely new concept in sound . . . it's so easy, a baby could learn to play it in fifteen minutes. All you do is put on your favourite record and play along with the group of your choice. The exciting sounds you make together will be unbelievable. Go along NOW to your local music or record shop and try one out. Take home a STYLOPHONE today and play with the groups TONIGHT.

IT'S ALL HAPPENING, THE CRAZE HAS BEGUN, EVERYBODY'S PLAYING THE STYLO-PHONE

If you have any difficulty in obtaining a STYLOPHONE — rush to the nearest phone and complain to: —
Dubreq Studios
275/281 Cricklewood
Broadway, N.W.2
Tel.: 01-452-0047 /9456

BOWIE – KING OF THE NEWLY INVENTED STYLOPHONE.

'Unwashed' has been seen as a commentary by Bowie on the side-effects of sudden success on his personal life. There is also an element of the prodigal son wreaking revenge on hostile forces. It's a very strange performance and, at one point, Bowie sings "I'm raving mad" as he laughs and chortles to himself. The piece is allowed to develop into a rather indulgent Bo-Diddley-style jam session, dominated by harmonica and guitar, but it's the kind of loosening up that he needed to get out of his system. There is even a parody of Marc Bolan's vocal style cropping up amid the thunder of guitars, something he would repeat even more directly on his next album.

'Letter To Hermione' is a welcome relief after the intensity of the previous performance – it's a touching, heartfelt love song with minimal accompaniment. The lyrics are clear and direct for once and serve as a response to the break-up of his relationship with Hermione Farthingale. It must have been rather alarming for her to receive such protestations of love through the medium of the local wireless station, juke box and record store.

Apart from 'Space Oddity' the highlight of the album is 'Cygnet Committee', an epic packed with lyrics that develop like Oscar Wilde's Ballad Of Reading Gaol or the ancient poem *Beowulf*. Perhaps not quite that deep and long-winded, but this is certainly an intriguing piece of work delivered in one exhausting but exultant "take".

In sharp contrast 'Janine' is a straightforward tune that shows that Bowie could easily have run a parallel career as a successful Country and Western singer.

'An Occasional Dream' is a pretty Beatle-style ballad with lots of acoustic guitars, which may have led to the claim in one TV documentary about his life that "he made a series of folk albums before he made *Ziggy Stardust*".

'The Wild Eyed Boy From Freecloud' is blessed with an imaginative title whjle 'God Knows I'm Good' is a more down to earth tale of an elderly lady caught shoplifting.

'Memory Of A Free Festival', a tribute to the Beckenham event, builds up to a wild climax in which Bowie chants with a strangely joyless frenzy "The Sun Machine is coming down and we're gonna have a party," almost as if he doesn't quite believe it. As with many of Bowie's songs and messages there is always room for doubt.

Bowie later recalled his work on the album: '"Space Oddity' is the only number to come out of that period that I still have a feeling for, and 'The Cygnet Committee' is the only other one."

The David Bowie album reached out to a slightly dazed and confused audience, bewildering those raised on 'The London Boys' or entranced by 'Space Oddity.' The perpetrator retreated to Beckenham to spend more time with his new girlfriend Angie and, together with Tony Visconti and guitarist Mick Ronson, began plotting his next move.

HERMIONE FARTHINGALE (CENTRE), DAVID'S GIRLFRIEND, WITH DAVID (LEFT) AND JOHN HUTCHINSON (RIGHT) IN THEIR GROUP FEATHERS (1969).

THE MAN WHO SOLD THE WORLD

Released	April 1971
Produced by	Tony Visconti
Recorded at	Trident Studios and Advision Studios, London
Musicians	David Bowie (vocals, guitar)
	Tony Visconti (electric bass, piano, guitar)
	Mick Ronson (guitar)
	Mick Woodmansey (drums)
	Ralph Mace (Moog synthesizer)

WIDTH OF A CIRCLE

ALL THE MADMEN

BLACK COUNTRY ROCK

AFTER ALL

RUNNING GUN BLUES

SAVIOUR MACHINE

SHE SHOOK ME COLD

THE MAN WHO SOLD THE WORLD

THE SUPERMAN

The 1967 summer of love had seen a blossoming of spiritual values amid a youthful desire for peace and harmony. Now the stripping away of sexual constraints and social barriers meant that many of its adherents were plunging headlong into a new, more dangerous freedom.

In the middle of all this social upheaval, the mild mannered Mod, who had previously seemed no more threatening than a neighbourhood hairdresser, now found himself thrust into the spotlight as the leader of a whole new movement. It was nothing so political as Gay Liberation. When David Bowie unveiled *The Man Who Sold The World* in the UK, in April, 1971, it was like a howl from the underground; a flashing signal to fellow members of a previously silent minority. Here was an album that was not merely groundbreaking in marketing terms. It was a strange and rather disturbing look into a world of altered images, where a young man could become a young woman, at least so the public were led to believe from the remarkable cover photograph of the artiste. It was also a place where sanity and madness intertwined in a series of songs of furious intensity. Songs that dealt in doom and despair, and hinted that salvation and redemption were only possible through the process of a psychic journey through mind and soul.

Maybe that journey could be conducted by the alluring figure pictured on the cover. Clad in a beautiful satin dress, the elfin figure is stretched languorously across a chaise longue, with the king of diamonds held between the limp fingers of one hand while the other hand quizzically scratches a cascade of wavy auburn hair that frames finely-chiselled facial features. Tight but delicate lips are on the verge of pouting. The rest of the pack of cards lies scattered on the floor. In 1971, liberated London was ready for this kind of "coming out".

Further a field there was panic and uncertainty. At least Bowie hadn't lost his sense of humour. As he explained to all who would listen he was wearing "a man's dress". Later reissues of the album featured Bowie in more masculine garb – tights and a shirt. Ironically this was altogether more revealing and sexy than the rather modest dress, which was intended as a tribute to the portrait paintings of the pre-Raphaelite artist, Dante Gabriel Rossetti.

The £300 "man's dress" was one of six Mr Fish designs, purchased for Bowie by his formidable new wife Angela Barnett. He took two of the dresses to America for his first promotional tour in January, 1971. The trip was arranged by Mercury in order to boost album sales – *The Man Who Sold The World* had already been rush-released in the US. If Bowie intended to shock the world, the dress certainly had the desired result. He was given a body search by the immigration authorities at the airport and allegedly had a gun pulled on him in Texas by a snarling redneck. The conveniently enraged

cowboy needn't have worried. As Bowie explained, the image cultivated on his album cover was "purely decorative, it's just theatre". Even so, it was felt that the rather tasteful photograph was too daring for the American public (or at least nervy record executives) and another cover was hastily substituted, one of three that would eventually adorn the album. The second was a cartoon drawing by Beckenham artist Mike Weller that showed Cane Hill hospital, where Bowie's half-brother Terry Burns was confined. Bowie had suggested the cartoon design as a joke, but was angry at this compromise. It was one of the factors that eventually led him to leave Mercury and sign a long-term deal with RCA – a label whose most important artist had been Elvis Presley. With Presley's popularity then in decline, the somewhat dubious idea was floated that 'The King' would be replaced by 'The Queen'.

Without the appropriate visa, Bowie was officially unable to perform during his US visit, but he did radio and press interviews and sneaked in one appearance in Chicago, thanks to the efforts of his record company. He also made his first visit to New York where, accompanied by Angie, he sported the Mr Fish dress and completed the ensemble by carrying a handbag. Considerably safer in this more liberal and receptive city, he met Lou Reed, Iggy Pop and Andy Warhol, thanks to an introduction set up by his manager Ken Pitt. Bowie had already begun listening to Lou Reed and the Velvet Underground's records and he finally met Reed and Iggy at Max's Kansas City. Such encounters had great significance for Bowie's future development. Without doubt, he also drew inspiration from a group of actors associated with Andy Warhol's Factory, who produced a show called Pork, but he had clearly developed his taste for theatricality, strong imagery and a more raunchy brand of rock music long before he visited the US.

The songs were as important as the visual shock tactics. These represented an outburst of anger against repression, and a rejection of middle-of-the-road pop music, fashions and attitudes that had bedevilled the career of the essentially non-conformist Bowie. As a youth originating from the uninspiring suburbs of South London, he'd had enough of playing by the rules. As he said: "In suburbia you are given the impression that nothing culturally belongs to you. You are in a waste-land and anybody with an iota of curiosity wants to escape and find who one is and find some roots. There is a desperation to get out, and an exhaustion with blandness."

This was the right time to fight blandness, to explode and assert his own ideas, values and feelings. Wearing a dress wasn't an expression of anything so mundane and conformist as being gay; the idea was simply to shock and amuse. Bowie didn't want to be the leader of a cause – he was more concerned

DAVID BOWIE IN HIS "MAN'S DRESS".

with expressing himself as an individual, although of course his sheer strength of personality and determination meant that he would become a leader of men, of women and of fashion. If anything, the pretty picture on the cover didn't do himself or the music justice. The songs on *The Man Who Sold The World* were hard, ironic, neurotic and even cynical. It came as a shock to all who had grown used to the cheeky, charming London boy and his apparently endless attempts to become a pop star. Now it seemed that David had become Bowie – threatening, unpredictable, dangerous and on the verge of becoming an icon, the rock star he always wanted to be. But he never again made an album with the same rock 'n' roll firepower, the intensity and sheer spontaneity that characterized *The Man Who Sold The World*.

DAVID WITHOUT HIS MR FISH DRESS FOR THE SECOND VERSION OF *THE MAN WHO SOLD THE WORLD*.

Work on Bowie's most magnificent and significant album so far began during April and May of 1970 at Trident Studios, in St Anne's Court, Soho, London and at Advision a few streets away. Trident was where The Beatles had secretly recorded most of *The White Album* and would later become the home of putative Glam group Queen. Bowie's album was put together under the aegis of the highly-creative, young, Brooklyn-born producer, Tony Visconti, who also played bass, piano and guitar with Bowie and helped with the arrangements. Engineer Ken Scott was another vital ingredient during the nail-biting process of recording, editing and mixing.

In the past, the term "pop producer" tended to suggest a rather uninterested figure, reading the racing results and desperate to get to the pub as soon as he could finish the session for that despised figure, "the singer". Bowie was fortunate to be working with a man who understood not only his musical ambitions, but his entire *raison d'etre*. Tony Visconti actually shared accommodation at Bowie's Beckenham home for a while and was fully cognizant of his creative process. He also found the singer frustratingly lethargic when it came to deadlines and productivity. Despite his propensity to dally with new wife Angela, when duty called Bowie was fired up by the highly-competent and effective hard rock outfit that had already begun the task of booting Bowie into the Seventies.

Bowie had begun to assemble his new band, which he called The Hype, in January, 1970. It included John Cambridge on drums and Tony Visconti on bass, later replaced by Trevor Bolder. Cambridge recommended guitarist Mick Ronson from Hull who had been playing in a Jeff Beck style with his band Rats.

Ronson had been to London and tried hard to break into the music scene but, unsuccessful, had been forced to return home and was now working as a municipal gardener. Ronson was urged to return to London and was recruited into the Bowie camp. He would become crucially important to the development of Bowie's future sound and image. The blunt-speaking Yorkshireman was the perfect alter ego to Ziggy Stardust, a down-to-earth antidote to the increasingly frenetic fantasy world evolving around him. Ronson was not initially interested in joining The Hype and was more than a little hostile to the idea of wearing make up and glittery clothes on stage.

After making a BBC broadcast, the new group made its public debut at the Roundhouse, Chalk Farm, as a support act for Country Joe And The Fish. Unprepared for their reception they were about to be given, each member of the band took to the stage in a different persona, with Bowie clad in spandex tights as Rainbow Man and Visconti, in white, as Hyperman.

Given the hippie habitués of the Roundhouse were supposed to represent the free thinkers of the day, the audience hostility came as something of a surprise. DJ and compere Jeff Dexter recalls: "It was the first time they had all dressed up and they got booed off." Most reports say this important show took place on February 22, 1970 at the Roundhouse. But Dexter insists Hype played on Wednesday, March 11, 1970, during a week of shows called "Atomic Sunrise" that incorporated live theatre and rock music. Dexter recalls that there was a tank of amyl nitrate on the stage. Occasionally a sponge was put into the tank and then wiped over members of the audience. Among the other artists in these shows were Marsha Hunt, Black Sabbath, Hawkwind and Quintessence. Dexter says David Bowie shared a billing with Genesis on the third night. "Why did the audience boo? Because they didn't like David doing the amateur theatrical stuff. It just didn't seem like rock 'n' roll. For a Roundhouse audience it just seemed too poppy and pretentious. I went and spoke to the audience and suggested they opened their minds a bit wider and tried to understand what David was trying to do. 'Everything's cool man. Just dig it!' I don't think David was really that upset."

Despite an apparently poor initial response, the new band was determined to carry on and Mick Ronson moved into the vast Bowie residence at Haddon Hall, Beckenham, where work continued apace on developing the songs and music for *The Man Who Sold The World*. John Cambridge was replaced by new drummer Mick "Woody" Woodmansey after Bowie complained rather brusquely about his playing. New arrival Woodmansey certainly brought a raucous, unfettered drive to proceedings, ideal for the creation of the "underground" sound.

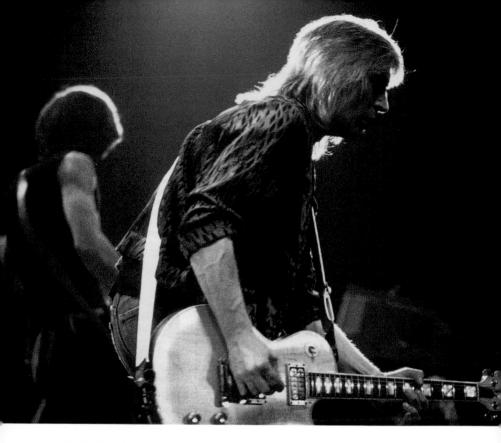

THE WIDTH OF A CIRCLE

The power of Bowie's band made immediate impact with this extraordinary eight-minute curtain-raising epic. Four decades later, 'Width Of A Circle' still retains its power to shock and entrance and, together with 'All The Madmen', remains one of the most important recordings in the canon of Bowie's work. What makes the piece so interesting, apart from the unexpected twists of the arrangement and intriguing lyrics, is the interaction between singer and musicians. Instead of attempting to dominate proceedings, or sing in a series of predictable verse and chorus routines, Bowie is, at times, almost swamped by the band's power.

He allows ideas to grow and multiply like some bacterial growth on a laboratory slide. Mick Ronson's cat-like guitar sets the scene with barely controllable outbursts before settling into a chunky riff, given extra strength by Visconti's unexpectedly sonorous bass. By the early Seventies Led Zeppelin

THE LATE MICK RONSON – A SPIDER FROM MARS.

and Black Sabbath were setting new standards of heaviness in mainstream rock. Yet there was something far more disturbing, even frightening, about the intensity of the Ronson/Bowie/Visconti triumvirate. By now Hype had evolved into a stronger, more adaptable outfit, with Ralph Mace, ostensibly an A&R man from Mercury Records, introducing the newly-invented Moog synthesizer. The team played with a savagery completely at odds with Bowie's supposedly fey image and yet much more appropriate to the depth of his new compositions.

The slight variations in the tempo and imperfections in the tuning during this particular performance may sound strange to modern ears, used to soulless, computerized accuracy. Yet it all adds to the darkly magical flavour. Stranger still is Bowie's voice – echoing, erratic, moving in a series of muttered asides, strangled outbursts and loud protestations, almost divorced from the band and yet an essential part of an increasingly crazed performance that has been described as an "hallucination with religious overtones".

"IT WAS THE FIRST TIME THEY HAD ALL DRESSED UP AND THEY GOT BOOED OFF."

JEFF DEXTER

As Bowie embarks on his psychic journey he sings: "I ran across a monster who was sleeping by a tree... I looked and frowned because the monster was me."

He also makes the discovery that "God's a young man too" as Ronson unleashes a tortured solo in which strings are bent and hammered in a relentless assault. A fragment of Bowie's acoustic guitar, previously taped and played backwards, leads to a chorus of vocal chants before the tempo is abruptly halved. Then a brisk military march begins and Bowie launches into a kind of satirical tirade of innuendo: "He swallowed his pride and puckered his lips... my knees were shaking my cheeks aflame... his tongue swollen with devil's love... I said do it again, do it again..."

It's hardly sexually ambiguous. The gay sex messages trumpet loud and clear. Homoerotica is rampant. Immersed in this passage is a kind of parody of A.A. Milne's verse "They're changing guard at Buckingham Palace, Christopher Robin went down with Alice" (from his 1924 book of children's verse *When We Were Very Young*). At least that was the interpretation placed by goggle-eyed fans on first hearing. Only later was it revealed in lyrics included on the inner bag of the vinyl version (re-issued in 1972) that Bowie was singing "You'll never go down to the Gods again" and not, as some thought, "You'll never go down on the Guards again".

Having met God in the Devil's lair, Bowie gives way to another violent Ronson guitar solo. The piece reaches a devastating climax with booming tympani drum beats setting the seal on a true Bohemian Rhapsody, created when Freddie Mercury's Queen were still in the wings. In the final ominous

27

moments Bowie warns that he has, himself, become a spitting sentry, horned and tailed and "waiting for you".

This extraordinary work has been interpreted as Bowie's own retrospective view of a road taken to fulfilment, in which he looks upon his other self in a spiritually-detached way. The lyrics refer to a blackbird advising him to take his instruction from the mystical Lebanese philosopher Khalil Gibran, whose tempting concept is that the young must cast off conventional morality and, ignoring warning cries of "turn around, go back", explore their own sexual fantasies. This might seem dangerously self indulgent if the aim is to express the ultimate in human individuality. Bowie seems to suggest that it is not a wise move to follow every philosopher or demigod's advice and example too closely.

If 'Width Of A Circle' sounds full, firm and focused, that was probably because it was the only tune Bowie had completed when he first went into the studio to cut the album. He then had to set about completing the rest of the material within a tight three-week schedule.

YOUNG PETER FRAMPTON, SCHOOL FRIEND AND THE "FACE OF '68".

These were the days before bands and artists were allowed three years to make an album, if they so desired. The deadline pressure would lead Mick Ronson to succinctly describe the process of recording the album as "a pain in the arse". Or a pain in the width of a circle perhaps.

ALL THE MADMEN

The composer revealed that he was going through one of the worst times in his life when he wrote and recorded this song. Composed while living in penury at Haddon Hall in Beckenham, Kent, Bowie had suffered the loss of his father and was undergoing the painful transition from working with his other father figure, manager Kenneth Pitt, to the more abrasive Tony Defries. More to the point, Bowie's half-brother Terry Burns was suffering from illness that required treatment during his stay at Cane Hill hospital, and so the lyrics are very much preoccupied with the theme of incarceration. Beginning with a simple acoustic guitar accompaniment, Bowie sounds preoccupied and disturbed himself as he sings "day after day they send my friends away to mansions cold and grey". Here the patient stands facing and talking to the wall but he is quite happy in his secure hospital wing. He is quite content because his fellow inmates are all clearly suffering from the same condition. Bowie's double-tracked schizophrenic voice sounds particularly chilling as he intones "day after day they take some brain away", a reference to lobotomy, the practice of making surgical incisions in one of the nerve tracts in the frontal lobe of the brain, made during the treatment of intractable mental disorders.

Wooden recorders pipe a sad lament before the piece changes into a thunderous and menacing bolero. Freedom is not a choice on offer for the inmates: "I'd rather stay here with all the madmen than perish with the sadmen roaming free". The message is reiterated while a relentless, hand-clapping chant dominates and Visconti's bass is left alone to pick up the melody as Bowie intones "Zane, Zane, Zane". There can be no better way of creating meaningful music than drawing from deep, personal experiences.

'All The Madmen' has more validity than all the carefully contrived fashionable rock chic in the world. Bowie did not forget or discard this important piece of work. It was released as a single in the US in December, 1970, as a promotional tool, and it was also brought back into service for his 1987 'Glass Spider' Tour.

BLACK COUNTRY ROCK

There is no greater rival than a best friend. David Bowie and Marc Bolan were friends and rivals – both had been Mods, both were witty in a self-mocking way, and both had deep-rooted insecurities and an inner strength. They also shared the same musical icons – from Elvis to Bob Dylan. Both desperately wanted to be stars, and indeed were stars, at least in their own eyes and among their small coterie of supporters, long before the rest of the world belatedly discovered them. As streetwise London boys they were destined to be soul mates. Yet there always existed that urgency to be, in Andrew Loog Oldham's phrase, "a winner". Bowie had already seen his school chum Peter Frampton become a star with The Herd. While Bowie was still bogged down with laughing gnomes, Frampton was being hailed by teen magazine *Rave* as "The Face of '68". And two years later Marc Bolan was lording it in the charts with major hits like 'Ride A White Swan', having converted his whimsical acoustic Tyrannosaurus Rex into the more electrifying – and infinitely more successful – T Rex.

Bolan, once nicknamed the bopping imp, had become a superstar. The feeling grew that he needed to be squashed if only to bring him back down to earth. Perhaps that was the mood in the Bowie camp when they created 'Black Country Rock'. What other explanation can there be for the mocking tone exemplified by the T-Rex-style guitar riffing and the blatant impersonation of Marc's trademark vocal whinnies in the final boogie rave-up. It all brings a bit of much needed levity to an otherwise sombre and neurotic outing. The fact that Tony Visconti was also working with T Rex, a group that was much more productive in terms of studio work than Bowie, must also have been a thorn in Bowie's side. Perhaps the Bolan put-on was Bowie's way of sticking his tongue out at the pair of them. 'Black Country Rock' was on the B-side of 'Holy Holy', a single released by Mercury in January, 1971, which failed to make an impression on the charts. The endless cycle of flop singles was a source of huge frustration for Bowie and his supporters.

AFTER ALL

"Oh by Jingo" is probably the most unlikely vocal chorus in the long history of hook lines and yet it perfectly complements the lugubrious theme and dainty rhythm that sets the scene for an apparently pessimistic, but contrite, message to his followers. As Bowie sings in sepulchral tones, a quasi fairground or circus mood is generated by what sounds like a calliope – a steam-driven organ. Bowie muses on the now-abandoned hordes of hippies, once his potential supporters. He sees them as face-painted trippy beings left over from the Summer of Love, who have to face up to the strange new world of the Bowie-driven Seventies. "I've borrowed your time and I'm sorry I called", he sings apologetically, adding "forget all I've said, please bear me no ill". This might have been a reference to his disenchantment with hippies after his experiment with the Arts Lab and Free Festival in Beckenham in August, 1969, where he was actually heard being quite rude to those organizers he thought were becoming capitalists – ironic when Bowie was already prophesying to friends that he would become a millionaire by the time he was 30. But the young and beautiful are allowed to be inconsistent.

He once said that he thought the hippies were all too middle class and that working class people had just as much to say in a creative way. However it was the latter who tended to boo and throw beer bottles at him. 'After All', and its message, continued to be relevant on those future occasions when Bowie made one of many sea changes and seemed in danger of alienating his followers. 'After All' was used as background music in the 1975 BBC TV Omnibus documentary *Cracked Actor*, made by Alan Yentob. It accompanied a view of heavily-made-up American fans queuing up to pay homage.

After all – the Glam Rockers, having supplanted the hippies as his greatest fans, were also in line for the chop.

RUNNING GUN BLUES

'Running Gun Blues' is a virulent anti-war diatribe that satirizes the gung-ho mentality of the warrior, and is actually based on the true story of a disturbed Vietnam veteran who gained a taste for killing that he could no longer control. Composed at a time when the Vietnam war continued to dominate the news, and was reaching a frenzied climax after more than a decade of continuous battle on the ground and in the air, this was more than just another protest song. It was the young and vigorous Bowie at his most ironic as he anticipated the kind of Rambo character loved by Hollywood movies – the gun-toting, invincible killer let loose on society in the name of democracy.

As the chord structure unfolds, over a long and unusual bass line, so Bowie intones the lyrics with a kind of manic precision and the humour of the asylum. "I count the corpses on my left, I find I'm not so tidy", he sings, then describes his warrior slashing at his victims, cracking their heads and bombing them from their beds. Even when the war is officially stopped by "peacefuls" he slips out with his rifle and plugs "a few civilians". It's the theatre of the macabre, as Bowie continues his murderous spree completely under the influence of the running gun blues. It's only a pity that the production lets down this potentially powerful piece. The drummer's crashing cymbals sound like they are two blocks away for all the effect they have. With no intended disrespect to Tony Visconti and Ken Scott, since they had the task of converting Bowie and the band's ideas on the hoof, it's a shame that these tracks weren't recorded by BBC sound engineers. The British Broadcasting Corporation's union men in brown coats made a good job of recording artists like Jimi Hendrix and The Yardbirds, as subsequent releases have proved. Indeed Bowie did make some recordings for the BBC, resulting in less gimmicks and better balance. It is known that he recorded over a dozen individual sessions for the BBC including such shows as *Sounds Of The Seventies* as well as concerts for John Peel and Dave Lee Travis when he featured such numbers as 'The Supermen', 'Ziggy Stardust', 'The Width Of A Circle', 'Wild Eyed Boy From Freecloud', and even 'The Cygnet

Committee'. But then it is the irrational, uneven, blitzkrieg of sound heard here that often gives these songs their edge. Bowie had tried the well-rehearsed session man route during the Sixties with his Deram recordings. In those days he had prepared all his lyrics and arrangements well before going into the studio. Now he was working out demos at home and in the studio with Visconti, Ronson and Woodmansey. If the results were haphazard, they were also very exciting.

SAVIOUR MACHINE

'Saviour Machine' is an inspired into a technological future in which Bowie sees a society where the wonders of science dominate everyone's lives to the point where their own intellect and efforts are sublimated. Viewed from the perspective provided by the Nineties, this now seems like a prophecy fulfilled. How the young Bowie would have loved the idea of the personal computer, the Internet and the mobile phone – indeed he would later become one of the first major music stars to embrace the Net, launching his own award-winning website. When he was recording 'Saviour Machine' back in 1970 British phone boxes still required the user to "Push Button A" to make a call, TV was in black and white and computers were vast machines rarely found outside of universities. The premise of the song is quite brilliant and, in an age when smart bombs are thought capable of influencing political events and human thought, the concept is not so far-fetched. Except that even the smartest missiles are still just a sign of human frailty and incompetence rather than omnipotence. And so any machine intended to provide salvation is doomed to failure as Bowie clearly predicts with this intriguing composition. His machine, as proposed by the mythical "President Joe" (see Reagan or Bush) would stop all war and provide food for the masses. Humanity loves the machine for its benevolence but the device itself becomes bored, and begs people to stop believing in machine logic. The warning is clear – life has become too easy and a plague (AIDS?) might be on the way.

The machine also threatens to bring back war and warns human-kind to send it away before it begins to wreak havoc. The message is simple: "You can't stake your lives on a saviour machine". Both attractive and remarkably prescient, 'Saviour Machine' gives the listener the eerie sense that we have only just arrived in David Bowie's future world, a time and space also anticipated by Arthur C. Clarke and Stanley Kubrick. Bowie's singing has strong overtones of the same Anthony Newley whose influence prevailed on earlier work. Bowie himself says: "Newley used to make his points with a broad Cockney accent and I decided that I'd use that now and again to drive a point home."

SHE SHOOK ME COLD

A heavy guitar intro, more Jimi Hendrix than Jeff Beck, sets the scene for a powerful sexual drama that delves into a pastiche of Cream-style heavy rock where bass, drums and guitar dominate proceedings. Bowie steps back to smoke a cigarette or two while the band jams and Visconti, in particular, makes a meal of his bass guitar work. It's the kind of freak-out that many a festival-goer might have endured sitting in the mud, while the Idiot Dancers literally had a field day. Those who thought Bowie's latter-day band Tin Machine was a new departure for the singer, should recall that he was

ZIGGY PLAYS GUITAR.

perfectly willing to take a back seat even during this pre-Ziggy period. Strangely enough, his absence from the microphone while the band goes wild, is still in itself significant. It is like a deafening silence. You know he is there. And his return for the final vocal chorus is taken with all the cool aplomb of a master, stubbing out his cigarette and taking his rightful place at the front, as the sweat-stained, exhausted players signal that he must return to save their sanity. Bowie's own sanity and virginity seem to be sacrificed on the altar of the nameless sex goddess he encounters in this spurting crescendo.

THE MAN WHO SOLD THE WORLD

Bowie's interest in Buddhism, and his fascination with the concept of reincarnation is expressed in this intriguing title song. Bowie's opening remarks make passing reference to the often-quoted lines by the American poet Hughes Mearns: "As I was going up the stair I met a man who wasn't there. He wasn't there again today. I wish, I wish he'd stay away." Here Bowie intones: "We passed upon the stair, we spoke of was and when although I wasn't there." Bowie thinks his friend on the stair died a long, long time ago but the vision explains that he is face to face with 'The Man Who Sold The World'. The man is, of course, his alter ego, which in this case can either be interpreted as a second self or a very close and intimate friend. It is noticeable that, although the recording techniques of the day were able to cope with the sound of a scraper adding percussion effects, once again the drums sound like they are in another room and the cymbals are apparently swathed in cotton wool.

Hailed as one of the most attractive and memorable melodies on the album, the song was covered in 1973 by Sixties pop singer Lulu. Bowie's brooding song was one of her first big hits since the distinctly unhip 'Boom Bang-A-Bang' in 1969, and helped raise her profile. Bowie, who respected Lulu from her days as an icon of early British R&B, not only produced the record but provided backing vocals and saxophone. In 1979 the song was revived by Bowie himself when he performed it on the popular US TV show *Saturday Night Live*, with Jimmy Destri of Blondie on keyboards. When the Nineties grunge era dawned and Bowie's star was in danger of being eclipsed by new bands such as Nirvana, Nirvana's singer, Kurt Cobain, paid tribute to Bowie by covering the song on the *Unplugged* album.

THE SUPERMAN

Like all well-read young men with a thirst for knowledge, Bowie became intrigued by the writings of German philosopher Frederick Wilhelm Nietzsche (1844-1900). In his work *Also Sprach Zarathustra* he developed the idea of the Superman. (Zarathustra is the Avestan name of Zoroaster, the Persian prophet.) In it he claimed that "Nothing is true, everything is allowed" and wrote that the suffering of slaves was insignificant and all higher culture was based on the intensifying of cruelty. As history showed, such ideas can have a disastrous effect – as they did when the Nazis interpreted them literally. It is worth noting that Nietzsche died after 12 years of complete insanity. Nevertheless, when the awesome Richard Strauss composition *Thus Spake Zarathustra* became one of the theme tunes from the classic movie *2001: A Space Odyssey*, it aroused great interest among the young in the writings of the notorious philosopher whose writings had, in turn, inspired the music. How much of Nietzsche and how much of Captain Marvel is in 'The Supermen' is a matter for debate. Nevertheless the concept provides a platform for some of Bowie's most vivid imagery. "No death for the perfect men. Life rolls into one for them" he explains. Mankind's potential for greatness is the pervading idea. The concept of male superiority was to be more fully explored when Bowie developed his concept of Ziggy Stardust, the omnipotent rock star. On the session that produced 'The Supermen' the drums were at last given the power to fit the theme and Bowie delivers his poetical stanzas with a manic intensity. This performance must surely have had a profound effect on fledgling singer Peter Gabriel, who adopted a similar kind of theatrical delivery for his own characterizations with Genesis, a band that Bowie supported on some of their early gigs. Bowie's performance on 'The Supermen' is mad, bad, and dangerous. And left his newly-won fans desperate for more.

FRIEDRICH WILHEIM NIETZSCHE, GERMAN PHILOSOPHER, POET AND INFLUENCE.

35

HUNKY DORY

Released	December 17, 1971
Produced by	Ken Scott
Recorded at	Trident Studios, London
Musicians	David Bowie (vocals, guitar, saxophone, piano)
	Mick Ronson (guitar, arrangements)
	Trevor Bolder (bass)
	Rick Wakeman (piano)
	Mick Woodmansey (drums)

CHANGES
OH! YOU PRETTY THINGS
EIGHT LINE POEM
LIFE ON MARS?
KOOKS
QUICKSAND
FILL YOUR HEART
ANDY WARHOL
SONG FOR BOB DYLAN
QUEEN BITCH
THE BEWLAY BROTHERS

DAVID (LEFT) WITH
HIS MOTHER MRS
MARGARET JONES
(CENTRE) AND NEW
WIFE ANGIE, OUTSIDE
BROMLEY REGISTRY
OFFICE ON THEIR
WEDDING DAY,
MARCH 20, 1970.

The early years of the seventies were a frantically busy and crucially important time for David Bowie. All the pent-up energy, ideas, plans and dreams that had been thwarted in the previous decade were now coming to fruition in a glorious out-burst of Bowie madness. As an astonished pop world looked on, Bowie the beautiful emerged like a butterfly from a chrysalis with his latest album *Hunky Dory*.

Even if it wasn't obvious to the outside world or to some of his closest advisers, Bowie had a master plan. Always a cool dude and somewhat secretive, he was ready to seize each new opportunity when the moment was right. Whatever he did during this period came as a surprise, especially to those who thought they had figured him out. Who would have thought the underground gay icon would get married? Yet he took the plunge and wed his girlfriend Angela at Bromley Registry Office on March 20, 1970. The daughter of an American engineer living in Cyprus, Mary Angela Barnett had been educated in Switzerland and New York and studied psychology at Kingston Polytechnic. She was undoubtedly a woman of the world. From then on, as Angie Bowie, she had a tremendous influence on the impressionable young lad's career and she became a celebrity in her own right.

His next move was less surprising and perhaps more predictable. Bowie took the first steps away from his old manager Ken Pitt to place his future in the hands of a more astute businessman, his then financial adviser Tony Defries. He then signed publishing deals and a new record contract that vastly improved his finances and ensured that, in time, he became the rock superstar that everyone had been expecting him to become. Bowie and Defries would eventually fall out, but, in the meantime, came the album that many felt was one of his best. Despite a few spaced-out oddities, it certainly contained some of his most intriguing and satisfying work.

Hunky Dory was written in the white heat of creativity at a time when Bowie was feeling relief at teaming up with his new manager. Defries took care of business, injecting the sense of power and authority needed to get the Bowie enterprise off the ground. If this meant becoming a rock 'n' roll "product" – well it was better than spending the rest of his life organizing hippie gigs and dabbling in Buddhism. All Bowie had to worry about now was writing songs, playing gigs with his musical playmates and buying some new frocks, or at least the best tailored trousers in town.

Bowie and Ken Pitt finally parted company in August, 1970, and Defries set up the new Mainman management company, with Bowie as his main artist. Urgent action was needed. Despite all the hype, *The Man Who Sold The World* had been a slow seller and this only exacerbated Bowie's sense of frustration. Defries went into overdrive and convinced RCA that, given the right promotion, Bowie would become the next big rock star and quite probably the biggest star on the label since Elvis Presley. CBS had been a contender, giving serious consideration to signing the "new" young English singer but senior executives were put off by his feminine image and by the dress worn on the cover of his Mercury album. In the end Bowie signed to RCA at their New York office in February, 1971. Around this time, while Bowie was on a promotional trip to New York, Bowie met and became firm friends with Lou Reed.

In London, during the summer, Bowie did some rare gigs and played a few of the songs that would appear on his next album, with his band, The Hype. He worked on the demos and, in June, Bowie and Angie's son Duncan Zowie Hayward was born. The same month Bowie gave a new song called 'Oh! You Pretty Things' to Peter Noone of Herman's Hermits fame, which became a Top 20 in the UK. This success, together with the demo tapes for Bowie's new album, set the seal on the deal with RCA. In July he began recording material for *Ziggy Stardust*, even before the new album, *Hunky Dory*, was released in December, 1971.

Instead of causing the expected sensation, *Hunky Dory* seemed destined to languish in the shops, even the first single, 'Changes', failing to dent the chart in the UK. Incredibly, it would be 1973 before any of the *Hunky Dory* tracks made it into the British singles charts.

The title of the album struck a strange note for those unfamiliar with the phrase. Some thought it was an old Cockney expression. In fact it was an outdated and long-forgotten Americanism that had been current in the Thirties or even earlier. "Everything is hunky dory" was the kind of thing you might hear in a light comedy starring Fred Astaire and Ginger Rogers. Indeed, the striking cover picture on the album showed Bowie looking like an old-time movie star with tinted blond hair. "He looks like Greta Garbo" snorted one cigar-chomping record executive. Hunky dory was simply an expression of approval to show that everything is satisfactory. "Hunky" came from the Dutch "honk" meaning a goal scored in a game and signified being in a good position. By the Seventies it was the sort of thing you might hear from a maiden aunt who hadn't been to the cinema for a while. In Bowie's hands, however, hunky dory was updated and overnight became the epitome of cool.

He certainly looked cool on the cover shots taken by Brian Ward. Apart from the tinted-blond movie-star pose on the front, the rear photograph showed an attractive, slim, long-haired youth in baggy flared trousers and clingy shirt that encircled a tiny waist. Bowie never looked more vulnerable and yet the songs had a remarkable strength. The hand-scribbled notes on the LP sleeve looked scrappy but they gave a personal feeling of communication with his listeners. Here was Bowie talking – and singing – directly to his fans. It was this on-going sense of involvement and identity that was crucial to his future success and elevation to superstardom.

Bowie credited his guitarist, somewhat grandly, as "Michael Ronson", responsible for the arrangements. His other musicians included Woody Woodmansey "Playing an excellent round of dr-dr-drums". Trevor Bolder was getting bolder on bass and Bowie's blond-haired mate, Rick Wakeman, and a veteran of the *Space Oddity* session, played the piano. With hindsight perhaps Rick should have stayed with the Bowie band and done the tours that later became the province of Mike Garson. He might have been happier as one of Bowie's fellow Spiders than slugging it out with Yes. Of himself, Bowie noted in self-deprecating tones: "I played some guitar, the saxophones and the less complicated piano parts." Sessions took place on familiar ground at Trident Studios in Soho with Ken Scott taking over from Tony Visconti, who had fallen out with Tony Defries.

Although in retrospect *Hunky Dory* has increased in stature with the passing years, at the time Bowie was anxious to press on with *The Rise And Fall Of Ziggy Stardust And The Spiders From Mars*. As Bowie explained much

JOLLY RICK WAKEMAN, KEYBOARD WIZARD WHO PLAYED ON *SPACE ODDITY* AND *HUNKY DORY*

later: "I wanted to take my time over that, so *Hunky Dory* was an interim project to get me through the recording contract, which meant that I had to have an album out. So I did *Hunky Dory* but I did about half the Ziggy album beforehand. When we were doing this album we felt flippant and flamboyant."

Bowie often gives the impression that he didn't actually like the record as much as the critics or the fans. He felt that some of the songs were too sweet or too simple and that it was all a rushed job, done before he could get down to more serious business. In fact the material showed a burgeoning skill and confidence and the songs were more rounded and "listener friendly". It was this album that finally encouraged doubters and waverers to take Bowie seriously. After this record appeared Bowie's career was assured and the singer never looked back.

"The album got a lot out of my system, a lot of the schizophrenia. *Hunky Dory* was a very worried album because I didn't know what I was supposed to be doing." Bowie expressed his concern that he still wasn't being accepted at home. "I dared to hope for too long about England, so I don't dare to hope for more. If I wasn't doing this I don't know what I'd do. I'd either be in a nuthouse or a prison."

As *Hunky Dory* went on sale at the beginning of 1972, so Bowie began to invest in a whole new range of stage clothes. He put together the kind of act

"I PLAYED SOME GUITAR, THE SAXOPHONE AND THE LESS COMPLICATED PIANO PARTS." DAVID BOWIE

that would impress a plane-load of US journalists flown to England to see him in action at a special concert, and hopefully send the good news back to the US. One of the press representatives was a reporter from Andy Warhol's *Interview* magazine.

However, it was a front page story in *Melody Maker*, and a revealing interview with journalist Michael Watts, which described him as camp and encouraged Bowie to admit he was gay, that opened the floodgates of publicity and controversy. It was a terrific boost for Bowie as the national press suddenly began to devote acres of column inches to the new star who wore a dress, make-up and dyed his hair red. Even so, in the summer of 1972, while Bowie was the talk of London, the top-selling albums in America were *Thick As A Brick* by Jethro Tull, *The Osmonds Live* and *Sammy Davis Jnr Now*. Clearly there had to be some changes made.

During 1972 Bowie went out on his first major tour for years, enthusiastically backed by the group that worked with him on *Hunky Dory*. Only now they were no longer called Rats or Hype – collectively, they were to be known as The Spiders From Mars. So the opening track on Bowie's fourth album seemed ever more blindingly appropriate and indeed its very name was attached to Bowie, whether he liked it or not. He would be the man who made changes a way of life.

CHANGES

"Ch-changes" stammers Bowie in the song that changed his world. It may not have been a chart success at home, but at least it got to Number 66 in the US. More importantly it signalled to those who would listen that Bowie was a master tunesmith. This was a song that grabbed the ear and stayed in the mind and should have been a smash hit. Released as a single, coupled with 'Andy Warhol' on the B-side in January, 1972, it got a lot of airplay and was heard in all the best clubs. It also gained Bowie the attention of the cognoscenti. For Bowie the song represented all the changes he had been through in his past life, and summed up his chameleon qualities. He sang "Every time I thought I'd got it made, it seemed the taste was not so sweet." These changes doubtless also related to his friends and associates as much as any peripheral changes in his own musical style and image – few artists had been through so many stages where the "closed for alterations" sign had gone up. The song also refers to changes on a wider scale, taking in his impressions of the turmoil and youth protest that he'd seen in America while the Vietnam war was at its height. "These children that you spit on... try to change their worlds" he fulminated.

Bowie later thought his creation was somewhat "neurotic" and would have preferred to have put 'Life On Mars?' out as a single but he left the decision up to RCA, who felt 'Changes' had a better chance. It was sufficiently simple and direct enough in style and content to appeal to DJs and to younger fans, while at the same time retaining that spark of genius that separated Bowie from all his Glam Rock rivals. The song has a masterful arrangement that still sounds very sophisticated and is blessed with some of Rick Wakeman's most mature and melodic piano work. What's more, the production is excellent and the vocal mix very clever, given the need to blend layers of backing vocals with a long and complicated lead line.

It may have been these subtleties, including the use of a saxophone tag at the end, that made it all too much for pop singles buyers currently being reared on T Rex. When Bowie sings the introductory "I still don't know what I was waiting for and my time was running wild..." and refers to "a million dead-end streets", he sounds like he is narrating a movie script, albeit one that is clearer and more meaningful than any number of hippie freak-outs. One of the most telling lines comes when he describes how he has often turned to face himself but has never caught a glimpse of how others "must see the faker. I'm much too fast to take that test". He describes himself rather unkindly as a faker on at least two occasions on the album. Another significant and prophetic phrase emerges at the climax of the song, where he warns rock 'n' rollers they are doomed to get older. "Time may change me but I can't trace time." In sending such messages he somehow distances himself from commitment to being a rock 'n' roller' himself, maintaining that position as the glamorous poseur with the freedom to change himself at will.

On a more practical note, Bowie reveals himself as a master of jazz phrasing when he slips into the verse, and this performance, in particular, shows that in technical terms alone Bowie was and remains streets ahead of his rivals. It was just a shame that on later albums such as *Young Americans* he would sublimate this fresh and dazzling vocal technique into the constraints of a cruder form of R&B. The odd thing is, that although his voice is instantly recognizable, there must be at the very least a dozen or so "Bowie voices" floating in the cosmos.

Just as 'Changes' was released as a single in January, Bowie played a one-off live show at the Lanchester Arts Festival near Coventry. At the time he had been swamped with offers of bookings, but had turned them all down. He simply thought Lanchester, with its intelligent student audience, was a better place to play than some lout-infested pub. "I've changed my whole outlook about live appearances," he told journalists at the time. "We're not going to go flogging around the country every night but we'll do much more live work than we have in the past. Having enthusiastic people around me makes life so much easier and it's made me more enthusiastic myself." At this rare 'Changes' gig he was accompanied by Ronson, Woodmansey and Bolder and the fans went wild. Bowie felt the electrifying atmosphere and said quietly: "I'm going to be huge and it's quite frightening in a way, because I know that when I reach my peak and it's time for me to be brought down, it will be with a bump." He needn't have worried. Within a few months "Bowiemania" saw thousands of fans being turned away from packed-out gigs across the country.

OH! YOU PRETTY THINGS

"Wake up you sleepy head, put on some clothes shake up your bed." On this lively song about the aspirations and importance of youth culture, Bowie promulgates the view that "pretty young things" would become the new "homo superiors" destined to be like supermen bent on taking over the world. This was Bowie's version of the song that he had given to Peter Noone, at the behest of pop mogul Micky Most. Noone's version was released in May, 1972, and stayed in the charts for a dozen weeks. It was Noone's finest post-Hermits hour. Here the striking piano introduction (which from the heavy choice of chords sounds more like Bowie than Rick Wakeman at work) builds up the tension before the band joins in the party with encouraging hand claps.

"Gotta make way for the homo superior" insists the composer, who appears in frisky Bolanesque mood, despite the air of Nietzsche-inspired schizoid intensity, which pervades the deeper reaches of the lyric. Like many of the songs on *Hunky Dory*, this sees Bowie wondering whether the latent potential of mankind can ever be fully realized. His own view seems to vacillate between doubt and optimism, the positive and the negative. He later said that the whole album was written "When I thought we still had a chance. "At this time in his life, he naturally saw the future as being full of hope. In 'Oh You Pretty Things' he still sees rock music as the means by which homo superior will triumph over the cavemen. The cavemen themselves probably preferred Black Sabbath, another band who used Rick Wakeman on their sessions!

EIGHT LINE POEM

More heavy piano chords support the curiously country-and-western-tinged vocal delivery that is employed here. The verse is interspersed with a few judicious cowboy guitar phrases from the surprisingly under-used Ronson. While not exactly earth-shattering or radio-friendly it's an intriguing interlude designed to provide food for thought. The cactus by the window? Even the greatest minds in rock have been defeated in their search for a meaning. In my view it could be a thinly-veiled reference to the cactus that takes on human form in science fiction story *The Quatermass Experiment*.

LIFE ON MARS?

The quest for life on the Earth's red-planet neighbour had been one of the great obsessions of the age. Then, just a few years after the appearance of Bowie's mysterious and appealing song, space probes revealed, sadly for romantics every-where, that there was no life on Mars and probably never had been. It was a dead planet, a desert with no canals, no monsters, not even a face. But until this grim news reached Earth, poets could still dream. Certainly Bowie, who had been a UFO buff, a sci-fi fan and had already written the definitive cosmic chart buster 'Space Oddity', was not averse to reaching for the stars to seek inspiration. But 'Life On Mars?' is more rhetorical than scientific or astronomical in its ambitions and it looks much closer to home. It is also one of the standout performances on the album and a classic of the pop genre that has probably never been equalled.

Rick Wakeman's deft touch at the keyboards is unmistakable as once again Bowie plucks a devastatingly gripping and original opening line about "the girl with the mousy hair". The very banality of this description quickly establishes that this is no jaunt into outer space. The girl has simply had a row with her parents and has gone to the cinema, only she's seen this picture before and is bored by the "Western" full of familiar scenes. Like the sailors fighting in the dance hall and lawman beating up the wrong guy. "Oh man!" Look at those cavemen go" groans Bowie at the predictable nature of base mankind – Homo Inferior indeed. Here is a song full of provocative images, of Mickey Mouse turned into a cow, of workers striking for fame. There's even a starry-eyed reference to John Lennon, the man who would one day record a song called 'Fame' with Bowie. Extraordinary how Bowie littered his songs with clues, premonitions and prophecies like the Nostradamus of jive. Despite all this dazzling array of images and the violence on the silver screen: "The film is a saddening bore 'cause I wrote it ten times before". The crucial cry "Is there life on Mars?" is a rhetorical question posed about the likelihood of real and active life ever impinging on those victims oppressed by the grinding inevitability of everyday existence.

It is an example of Bowie at his most thoughtful – both he and the girl of his creation muse on the possibility that the meaningless violence of life on Earth has become both a sort of freak show and also entertainment for extra-terrestrials of a higher intelligence. At least the civilized beings of Earth could share the joke with their Martian neighbours. As the strings and *2001*-style tympani crash to a climax, a studio telephone can be heard ringing and a voice mutters "mind the phone". If the space telephone rings, don't answer.

KOOKS

Here is a jolly pop song that almost reverts back to the Mod era of Swinging London. Ideal accompaniment for an Austin Powers movie, it has an amazingly jaunty tune complete with Herb Alpert-style trumpet licks and some pub piano that only Wakeman could have played so well. You can almost imagine the pints of lager slopping over the keys. It's an example of the carefree attitude that Bowie described as being rampant in the recording studio. It's certainly a far cry from the frantic rock that would permeate his next album. Even so this tale of preparations for the new baby – young Zowie – and the couple of kooks who would be his parents, is both touching and amusing. Bowie even offers some warning about the perils of school days that lie ahead that are drawn from his own experiences. "Don't pick fights with the bullies or the cads, 'cause I'm not much cop at punching other people's dads."

He later confessed to being rather embarrassed about this delightful interlude, wincing: "This is how slushy and sentimental a songwriter can get." Even so, the lines about buying things to keep the baby warm and a funny old crib on which "the paint won't dry, I bought you a pair of shoes a trumpet you can blow" can still strike chords with parents everywhere. And just in case anyone had missed the point, Dad wrote "for small Z" in tiny letters on the record sleeve. In later years when Zowie, better known as Joe, heard the song he pointed out to Bowie that when the subject of homework came up he had once been advised to "throw it on the fire".

QUICKSAND

After the innocent joys of the surprisingly popular 'Kooks', the final track on side A of the original vinyl album returns once again to intensity, depth and adult preoccupations. There are contrasting references to such powerful figures as the black magician Aleister Crowley, the Nazi brute Heinrich Himmler, and even England's beloved Winston Churchill.

It was during David's sojourn in Los Angeles some years later that it began to be rumoured that Bowie had started to study the work of that arch-magician Crowley rather too closely. However, he would often talk about such matters in interviews more as flight of fancy or simply as a joke. On 'Quicksand' he expresses fear at the impending loss of power and tells his listeners he is torn between light and dark as he sinks into the quicksands of his thought. "Don't believe in yourself", he says, oddly at variance with the usual practice of telling the weak and unfortunate that they should believe in themselves. He lapses into a kind of Ray Davies rap from 'I am the Apeman' as he sings that he is not a prophet or a stone age man, just a mortal with the potential of a superman. It's that Homo Superior theme again, "Knowledge comes with death's release" he adds, somewhat ruefully, as the negative mode overwhelms him once more and Wakeman earns his bus fare home with a massive overtime bonus.`

"HAVING ENTHUSIASTIC PEOPLE AROUND ME MAKES LIFE SO MUCH EASIER AND IT'S MADE ME MORE ENTHUSIASTIC MYSELF."
DAVID BOWIE

FILL YOUR HEART

47

Somewhat cryptically, Bowie wrote in his sleeve notes: "Mick and I agree that the 'Fill Your Heart' arrangement owes one hell of a lot to Arthur G. Wright and his prototype." It also owes a lot to Paul McCartney and The Beatles. This strange ditty must have caused consternation in the offices of RCA, New York branch, at the first play-back session. You can almost imagine ashen-faced execs sending out for bagels and paracetamol as Bowie whoops and warbles his way through an incomprehensible piece of whimsy. It's actually a cover version – a rare thing on an early Bowie album. The song, by American singer/ songwriter Biff Rose, who was gaining some popularity at the time, is a paean of praise to the spiritual freedoms and therapeutic properties of leading the clear life of a genuine hippie. Heard against 'Quicksand', it offers an alternative philosophy to the dark arts and all their perils. Wakeman wraps it all up with a finale that would have delighted Chas & Dave.

ANDY WARHOL

Bowie was delighted when he once visited Warhol in New York to find that the exit from the elevator on Warhol's floor was blocked off by a brick wall. It somehow summed up the impenetrable nature of the artist. More interesting was Warhol's penchant for making stars out of nonentities. The whole idea of

fame was reduced to cameo roles for the ungifted and he felt that everyone should have their 15 minutes of fame. Manipulation was the name of the game and all this was a huge influence on Bowie's own thinking. Many years later, in 1995, Bowie actually played Warhol in a film, wearing the leather jacket and wig that were Warhol's stock-in-trade.

His tribute starts with a bit of studio fun comprising a debate between producer Ken Scott and Bowie about the correct pronunciation of "Warhol". Bowie laughs sweetly as he points out it isn't "Andy Warho".

Scott: "This is Andy Warho and it's take one."

Bowie: "It's Warhol actually."

Scott: "What did I say?"

Bowie: "'Ho' ...It's 'hol' as in 'holes'."

It may have been the banter that upset the real Andy Warhol, who apparently hated the piece, which had been intended as a tribute to his hugeness. It's impossible not to join in the laughter as the lads mock the name of someone who clearly thought he was the bees knees. "Andy Warhol looks a scream!" is the cry. He is described as dressing up his friends for show and letting people into his brain "Two new pence to have a go". Bowie blithely rubs it in by describing the Campbell's canned soup man as "Think about paint and the colour blue – what a jolly boring thing to do." Warhol clearly didn't like being reduced to a comic stereotype, even if Bowie's well-meaning spoof tries to capture the essence of cute that lay behind Warhol's art. After a spot of suitably surreal Spanish guitar from Ronson, the burst of applause in the empty studio must have been the final straw for a bruised ego.

SONG FOR BOB DYLAN

49

'Song For Bob Dylan' was the second of cheeky young Bowie's tributes to the great men in his life and, like Warhol, Bob Dylan didn't like his tribute. Bowie refers to him as "Robert Zimmerman", which may have upset him and the line about him having a voice like sand and glue was a trifle near the mark. And who likes having the tables turned on them? This does dangerously veer towards parody but it's meant as a heart-felt tribute and Ronson's guitar is very appropriate. The song is actually a call to Dylan to return to writing songs for the "revolution" and to scour his scrap-book for inspiration if the muse is not upon him. In a way Bowie is echoing Dylan's own plea to his mentor, Woody Guthrie, called 'Song For Woody'.

QUEEN BITCH

Mick Ronson instantly enlivens 'Queen Bitch', bursting back into action with some great rock 'n' roll guitar. One of the highlights of *Hunky Dory*, this is one track to give the A&R men a relief from their diet of painkillers. Here is the third of Bowie's heart-felt tributes. If anybody deserved a tribute it was Bowie himself, a far deeper, more sensitive, creative human being than any of those self-centred New York cab drivers. Bowie's "Oh yeah" as Ronson kicks in sounds very spontaneous and meaningful. It's a cheeky tale of gay love and

LOU REED, STAR
OF THE VELVET
UNDERGROUND.

cross-dressing in the nightclubs of Babylon – or possibly East Finchley. "I could do better than that" chortles Bowie disparaging the "bibbety bobbity hat" worn by the despised rival.

This track was later added as the B-side to 'Rebel Rebel' when it was released in February, 1974. On the album sleeve notes Bowie wrote next to 'Queen Bitch' "Some VU white light returned with thanks." This was a reference to the influence of The Velvet Underground and their song 'White Light White Heat' on this sharp and witty performance. It all seemed terribly daring at the time, and retains its hip charm, 30 years later.

THE BEWLAY BROTHERS

A magnificent piece of work, it's hard to believe this is on the same 12 inch disc (or CD) as 'Kooks' and 'Fill Your Heart'. Back in 1972, few people were aware that David Bowie had a half-brother, let alone one who was suffering from illness – so this simply seemed an obscure lyric, no stranger than any of Bowie's other coded messages. But this song dealt with the relationship of a brother whose fate was to wander abroad, neglected, and who eventually died in tragic circumstances. Background knowledge now puts 'The Bewlay Brothers' in a new light.

It begins with the sound of Bowie's chair creaking and his intake of breath as he readies himself to sing a difficult and important piece of introspection and self-analysis. The snatch of double-tracking adds to the mysterious atmosphere, as the spartan acoustic guitar prompts a stream of consciousness. The words flow as if read from a diary trans-muted into a poem. "We were so turned on", repeats Bowie wistfully. "My brother lays upon the rocks he could be dead".

A strange muttering chorus sounds like a frightening imitation of his real life brother coming back to haunt him and speaking in the slurred speech of the disturbed: "I'm starving for me gravy. Leave my shoes and door unlocked, I must just slip away, just for the day." It all becomes a cacophony of mutterings "Please come away", the voices distorted and fading over an insidious mumbling theme. Bowie is torn between loyalty to his brother and the need to escape himself. It all becomes more frightening and psychologically disturbing than a Hitchcock movie. For those who set great store by the sometimes overlooked and less fashionable *Hunky Dory*, this track is not just one of its most important moments, it is a key to the mystery of the man himself. Bowie, in a rare pronouncement on a song that was never performed in public said: "It's another in the series of David Bowie confessions."

More songs were intended to be included on the original album, or at least set aside for a companion piece which never actually materialized. They included 'He's A Goldmine', 'Bombers', 'Star Man', 'Round And Round', and 'Something'. When *Hunky Dory* was first reissued on CD, in 1990, the bonus tracks included 'Bombers', a different version of 'The Supermen', a demo of 'Quicksand', and an alternative version of 'The Bewlay Brothers'.

Whatever the reaction at the time and the lack of instant hits, the verdict of history is that Bowie's rushed "filler" album is very cool and, if you'll pardon the phrase, hunky dory.

THE RISE AND FALL OF ZIGGY STARDUST

AND THE SPIDERS FROM MARS

Released	June 6, 1972
Produced by	David Bowie and Ken Scott
Recorded at	Trident Studios, London
Musicians	David Bowie (guitar, saxophone and vocals)
	Mick Ronson (guitar, piano and vocals)
	Trevor Bolder (bass)
	Mick Woodmansey (drums)

FIVE YEARS

SOUL LOVE

MOONAGE DAYDREAM

STARMAN

IT AINT EASY

LADY STARDUST

STAR

HANG ON TO YOURSELF

ZIGGY STARDUST

SUFFRAGETTE CITY

ROCK 'N' ROLL SUICIDE

53

David Bowie's fifth, and perhaps most famous, album was devised during a highly productive and creative period.

It was also a time of nervous energy, when Bowie's position urgently needed to be consolidated, to ensure future fame and to boost his reputation. He came up with a masterstroke, but his career was still balanced on a knife-edge of uncertainties. The character of Ziggy Stardust remains a brilliant synthesis of influences and images. Yet the whole idea could have been a failure. Not everyone agrees that this still-controversial collection of songs contains his best work.

Despite smoother, more economical production and Bowie's focus on a highly imaginative and seductive concept, a lot of this album's music lacks the rock 'n' roll spontaneity of 'Space Oddity' or the neurotic intensity of *The Man Who Sold The World*. There is the feeling that Bowie the actor is taking over from Bowie the singer/song-writer. And maybe that is Ziggy's fault. As Bowie explained to writer Timothy White in 1990: "I took the idea of fabrication and how it had snowballed in popular culture. Realism and honesty had become boring to many jaded people by the early Seventies. I think the band only half understood what I meant, but I thought it would be such great fun to fabricate something so totally unearthly and unreal and have it living as an icon. So the story of Ziggy came out of that thinking. A lot of it came out of my own problems. It was a way of creating myself."

The Rise And Fall Of Ziggy Stardust And The Spiders From Mars is a wonderfully portentous title. As such it ranks alongside *Sgt Pepper's Lonely Hearts Club Band*, *Their Satanic Majesties' Request* and *Tales From Topographic Oceans*. This after all was the great age of the concept album. More importantly, the Ziggy album represents a kind of watershed in the way pop music looked at itself. The characterization of Ziggy as the ultimate rock star, armed with his fictional band The Spiders From Mars, is Bowie at his most detached and theatrical.

When Bowie invented Ziggy, it was the first time a rock artist had dared to take on the mantle of celebrity and examine it in such a ruthlessly calculated way. Ziggy Stardust became not just the focal point of an album but the centre-piece of an elaborate stage show and on-going media sensation.

As Bowie developed the Ziggy look with dyed red hair, tight pants and boots, he created the ultimate androgyne, an outrageously beautiful creature whose shock appeal was instantly enhanced when the singer told *Melody Maker's* Michael Watts in a famous interview "I'm gay, and always have been." It was a moment of madness.

Once the Ziggy movement got underway it proved a sort of community spirit among his followers glad to replace the hippie idealism of yore. "I'm with David Bowie – Aren't You?" became the slogan of the day as scores of Ziggy look-alikes burst out of their suburban closets.

The Michael Watts interview put the seal of success on Bowie's Ziggy Stardust master plan. Although Ziggy had everything Bowie needed, in the ensuing months it seemed he had created a Frankenstein's monster that would take him over and ultimately wreak revenge, if Bowie didn't destroy it first.

The origins of Ziggy have been pored over for years, yet for all its supposed influence and innovation, the Ziggy concept is only alluded to in the vaguest terms on the album – the story is hard to follow and the songs are not linked in any coherent fashion.

The saga of the space-age rock star had been assembled and mulled over some time before Bowie had actually become a star. When Ziggy burst on the scene many assumed the inspiration for the character was Marc Bolan, the self-styled Metal Guru. But Bowie's choice of Ziggy honoured Iggy Pop, the crazed Detroit-born front man of The Stooges. As a jazz fan, Bowie would also have known that Ziggy was a popular nickname among American musicians. Trumpet player Ziggy Elman, for example, was famed for his hot solos with the Benny Goodman Orchestra. For these reasons it was hard for some of the

"I WANT TO GO OUT LIKE VINCE TAYLOR. HE WAS THE INSPIRATION FOR ZIGGY."

DAVID BOWIE

music business fraternity to take Ziggy Stardust and his assorted Spiders quite as seriously as the Bowie camp intended. Nevertheless it was Ziggy who helped consolidate Bowie's grip on the public's imagination and ensured he would become the rock legend that Mr Stardust was intended to depict.

Several real-life characters had to be in place before this work could be completed. There was Angie, Bowie's wife, always ready to goad him into action and encourage a new hairstyle, and hairdresser Sue Fussey gave him his new look. They tried green before finally settling on red, a colour inspired by one of the red-haired models seen sporting the Kabuki-influenced clothes of Japanese designer Kansai Yamamoto, who was visiting London at that time. Later on, Kansai made all the stage clothes for Bowie and the Spiders From Mars for their early shows.

Tony Defries, Bowie's manager, could take off the business pressure and leave him free to concentrate on art, music and recording. Mick Ronson and pals could provide the Spidery backing and Ken Scott was on hand to replace the now-departed Tony Visconti at the mixing desk. The countdown had begun and Bowie cast about him for ideas.

It seems that the inspiration for Ziggy Stardust was not so much Marc Bolan as Ronald "Vince" Taylor, a long-forgotten early rock 'n' roll singer whose extraordinary story and fate had fired Bowie's imagination. An Englishman who moved to the US and later based himself in France, Taylor enjoyed a career in the early Sixties as the main rival to French pop hero Johnny Halliday. He remained a mythical figure in England, where he was often confused with Vince Eager. One of his best-known tracks was 'Brand New Cadillac', a B-side to his 1959 single 'Pledging My Love', and later covered by The Clash. He also had a UK hit with a song significantly titled 'I'll Be Your Hero' coupled with 'Jet Black Machine' which got to Number 15 in September, 1960.

Unfortunately for Vince, success in France turned his head and encouraged delusions of grandeur. He began to preach from the Bible on stage and act in such a wild, destructive fashion, that he claimed to be the Jekyll and Hyde of rock. In 1966 Bowie actually met him in London's Tin Pan Alley – Denmark Street – and somewhat nervously formed the impression that here was the ultimate crazed rock star. He heard how Vince would go on stage in white robes and tell audiences that he was Jesus Christ. Although neglected and ignored in the aftermath of these excesses, there is the probability that Bowie still had Vince Taylor in mind when he began thinking about Ziggy.

Taylor died in 1991 and Bowie remarked: "I want to go out like Vince Taylor. He was the inspiration for Ziggy. Vince was slowly going crazy. Finally

he fired his band and went on stage one night in a white sheet. He told the audience to rejoice, that he was Jesus."

There were other elements that made up the proto-rock idol. The rock world was only just coming to terms with the loss of burnt-out innovators Jimi Hendrix and Jim Morrison. The androgynous Mick Jagger and spaced-out Syd Barrett of Pink Floyd were also cast into the melting pot. As well as these musicians there was the ultimate Pop Art creation, Andy Warhol, with his dark glasses and blond wig. In Bowie's view, Warhol embodied the idea of the starmaker, a man who indulged in Svengali-like manipulation.

The Warhol influence came closer to home when the cast of *Pork*, a stage show based on life at Warhol's HQ, The Factory, came to London. The show featured Cherry Vanilla and Wayne Country and when they performed at the Roundhouse in Chalk Farm their antics, dyed hair and copious use of glitter made an impression on Bowie. The *Pork* people weren't impressed when they saw Bowie turning up for solo acoustic gigs in his old hippie gear, but he was already working on a new look that would out-*Pork* them all. He had already made an attempt at inventing a group in London, just as Warhol had sponsored Lou Reed and The Velvet Underground in New York. Bowie had launched a fashion designer called Freddi Buretti as "Rudi Valentino" and planned to record him with a new group called Arnold Corns. In April, 1971, he began recording anonymously with Arnold Corns and produced two singles for the

MICK RONSON (LEFT), BOWIE AND THE SPIDERS FROM MARS.

B&C label. The first featured Bowie singing 'Moonage Daydream' and 'Hang On To Yourself', both rerecorded by Bowie for the Ziggy album. The second was 'Hang On To Yourself' with 'Looking For A Friend' sung by Valentino.

Sadly, both records flopped and no more was heard of Arnold Corns, although the backing musicians included future Spiders Mick Ronson, Woody Woodmansey and Trevor Bolder. The Spiders of course had previously been Mick's group The Rats from Hull. Bowie recalls: "Ronson said: 'I've got these great guys up in Yorkshire that would be just great for playing with you' and I said 'Let's bring them down!' The whole idea of the album came first and the Rats became the Spiders later." The cast of Spiders included Bowie (guitar, sax and vocals), Mick Ronson (lead guitar, piano and vocals), Trevor Bolder (bass), and Mick Woodmansey (drums).

By the time recording began at Trident Studios in Soho, Bowie already had a bunch of songs ready and a good idea of what he wanted to do, although producer Ken Scott later said that there was no discussion about deliberately making a "concept" album. The sessions were underway even before Bowie's fourth album Hunky Dory had been released, which shows the kind of energy flow Bowie now summoned. He had started writing during the summer of 1971 and recording was done very quickly.

Mick Ronson and Ken Scott liaised on converting Bowie's ideas into musical reality, while the drummer and bass player laid down their tracks and left Scott to do all the mixing. The first version of the master tape, produced by December 1971, had a somewhat different track listing to the final product. It included versions of Chuck Berry's 'Round And Round' and Jacques Brel's 'Amsterdam' together with 'Velvet Goldmine' and 'Holy Holy', a song that had already been released as a single in January, 1971. The remaining items were 'Five Years', 'Soul Love', Moonage Daydream', 'Hang On To Yourself', 'Ziggy Stardust', 'Star' and 'Lady Stardust'. At one stage even the album's title was a different one – it was going to be called Round And Round.

In January, 1972 the band cut three more songs including 'Starman' 'Suffragette City' and 'Rock 'n' Roll Suicide'. Eventually the track listing for the album was complete with 'Starman' included to placate the record company's need for a single, and 'Round And Round' placed in the recycle bin. Bowie told an American interviewer at the time: "'Round And Round' was the kind of number Ziggy would have done on stage. Our enthusiasm for it waned after we heard it a few times. We replaced it with 'Starman' and I don't think it's any great loss."

When the Ziggy Stardust album was reissued on a Rykodisc CD in 1990 it included five bonus tracks including one called 'Sweet Head', which wasn't included on the original vinyl album because it's subject matter – oral sex. From this process of restructuring it can be seen that Ziggy was not intended to be a concept album. Bowie admitted it was a fractured piece of work and that there were only a few scenes depicting the Ziggy Stardust band. Indeed, the whole idea began to grow the more he talked about it and it gained momentum when he went on the road with the theatrical show that unleashed Ziggymania.

Almost as important as the music is the cover. A colour-tinted picture shows a camp-looking Bowie in blonde hair, purple boots and green jump suit, posing with a guitar in a back alley amid piles of cardboard boxes. He is standing under an illuminated sign for K West, a furriers based in Heddon Street. The back cover shows a glamorous Bowie, hand on hip, standing inside a traditional red London telephone box.

The album caused a sensation when it was released on June 9, 1972. It sold 8,000 copies in the first week alone and *Melody Maker* proclaimed a "A Star Is Born" when Bowie appeared on stage with Lou Reed at a special concert. The Ziggy look was presented to screaming fans during two nights featuring Bowie and his band at the Rainbow Theatre London on August 19 and August 20, 1972, the start of a full UK tour. On the opening night, Roxy Music played the first set and then the stage was cleared for Bowie's entrance, accompanied by music from Stanley Kubrick's *A Clockwork Orange*. He came out, amid clouds of smoke, looking like an android clad in a silver suit, his hair now bright scarlet, his white face highlighted with mascara. "Hello, I'm Ziggy Stardust and these are the Spiders from Mars," he chirped.

During the show that followed he frequently changed costumes, leapt around a stage set devised from scaffolding, and was joined at the climax of an extraordinary show by his old mime mentor Lindsay Kemp, dressed as a fairy angel and supported by the Astronettes dance troupe. One of the most memorable moments came when Bowie took off the silver suit and appeared in red underwear on the highest platform striking poses, while bathed in soft lighting. As he launched into 'Starman' a glitter ball began to revolve, casting its beams over an awe-struck audience. In the final moments of a wild, balletic freak-out, with Bowie arching his limbs like Rudolf Nureyev, there was a stunned silence. Then a lone voice bawled out "More!" And the audience was jolted out of its trance to give a wild ovation.

Watching the show were fellow stars Alice Cooper, Lou Reed, Elton John and Mick Jagger. Lou Reed later described Bowie's extravaganza as "Amazing, stupendous, the greatest thing I've ever seen." Bowie recalls: "It was the last of our real mixed media shows because we were using film footage,

PLEASED TO SEE
YOU? ONE-EYED
BOWIE GETS IT ON.

59

scaffolding, the Lindsay Kemp Mime Company and pre-recorded tapes." He forgot to mention the red underwear.

In September, Bowie began a US tour that climaxed with a sell-out concert at Carnegie Hall, New York on September 28, 1972, which won him glowing reviews. On November 24 his 13th single 'The Jean Genie'/'Ziggy Stardust' was released and the US tour finished with more Ziggy shows in Philadelphia (December 2, 1972). Although not all the shows were sell-outs, and there was still work to be done in selling the Ziggy/Bowie package to American audiences, it was undoubtedly a turning point in Bowie's life.

As he said later, somewhat ruefully: "I wasn't at all surprised 'Ziggy Stardust' made my career. I packaged a totally credible plastic rock star, much better than any sort of Monkees fabrication. My plastic rocker was much more plastic than anybody else's."

ZIGGY, IGGY AND (LOU) REEDY, LONDON 1972.

FIVE YEARS

Given the passion and sincerity, not to mention the anguish and dark humour, at the core of much of Bowie's earlier work, there is some-thing disturbingly and deliberately fake about many of these 'Ziggy' performances. The lyrics and the delivery just don't ring true and this is an example of a particularly mannered and even irritating song.

Bowie's voice, high-pitched and filled with Lennon inflections, meanders through the heavy string arrangement, which has overtones of 'I Am The Walrus'. The piece is intended to set the scene for the story of the mythical Ziggy Stardust and his contacts with beings from outer space. It is revealed that the world is dying and only has five years left before the end of the planet. This idea was quite prevalent at a time when environmentalists were spreading stories of the Earth's resources running out in just a few years. There are scenes of panic as news of impending doom hits America and even the TV newsreader weeps in despair, while Bowie observes an old friend drinking milk shakes in an ice-cream parlour, smiling and waving. Bowie later attempted to explain the scene: "It has been announced that the world will end because of lack of natural resources. Ziggy is in a position where all the kids have access to things they thought they wanted. Ziggy was in a rock 'n' roll band and the kids no longer want rock 'n' roll. There's no electricity to play it."

SOUL LOVE

'Soul Love' has a good deal of reedy saxophone playing from Bowie. There is, however, a good guitar solo from Mick Ronson and Bowie provides backing vocals with some help from Ronson. The piece is intended to put a religious spin on the world-facing-doom situation and stresses the importance of the many forms of love; a mother for a dead son, a boy for a girl, and a priest for the word of God. Although the composer himself feels he is no longer capable of giving love, he finds the capacity of others to express such feelings inspirational. However high-minded it does not bear much relevance to the story and the song was rarely performed live, except during a 1973 US tour. There is also a version of 'Soul Love' to be found on the live Stage (1978) album along with versions of 'Hang On To Yourself, 'Ziggy Stardust', 'Five Years', and 'Star'.

MOONAGE DAYDREAM

"I'm an alligator, I'm a mama papa comin' for you", sings Bowie, jumping straight into Bolan-style rock 'n' roll lyrics. It's pretty corny stuff but years later many long-in-the-tooth Bowie fans claimed that this was still one of their favourite numbers. This is the point in the story where Ziggy himself comes into play. The song was previously recorded by Arnold Corns (1971) and re-emerged here with revamped, heavily Americanized lyrics and strings added by Ken Scott during mixing. When Bowie performed 'Moonage Daydream' during his first American tour in 1972, he announced the number as if it had been written by Ziggy Stardust himself. 'Moonage Daydream', Corns-style, appears on the 1990 CD reissue of *The Man Who Sold The World.*

STARMAN

One of the best and most appealing songs on the album, 'Starman' was included as an after-thought at the behest of Dennis Katz, A&R man at RCA's New York HQ. Bowie had delivered the song to the label, intending it to be his next single and it was put on the album to ensure it received radio play. Another tale about a space traveller from the cosmos, it has a strong, catchy melody with a memorable chorus that "leaps from the speakers" as record reviewers were once prone to say. "There's a starman waiting in the sky, he'd like to come and meet us but he thinks he'd blow our minds," Bowie sings in best Judy Garland 'Over The Rainbow' mode, while the Starman interrupts radio broadcasts and advises Earthlings to "Let all the children boogie". Ziggy himself is supposed to have written the story of the Starman's coming, having been advised of the impending arrival in a dream.

'Starman', coupled with 'Suffragette City', was released as a single on April 28, 1972 and subsequently reached Number 10 in the UK charts three months later – Bowie's first hit in three years. Curiously, in spite of RCA's enthusiasm it was not a big hit in America, stalling at Number 65 in the charts. At home, however, the success of 'Starman' enabled manager Tony Defries to request a spot on BBC TV's *Top Of The Pops*, giving Bowie the national exposure he still needed. Incredibly at this time, Bowie was still playing low-paid gigs booked months before, earning as little as £150 a night.

As Bowie says: "'Starman' can be taken at the immediate level of 'there's a starman in the sky saying boogie children' but the theme is that the idea of things in the sky is really quite human and real and we should be a bit happier about the prospect of meeting people."

IT AIN'T EASY

There has been some confusion about this piece, which many thought was written by Ray Davies of The Kinks – even though it clearly states on the label that the composer is Ron Davies, an American writer whose work Mick Ronson had heard. This had originally been recorded during 1971 as a contender for the *Hunky Dory* album and doesn't seem in any way relevant to Ziggy. It's an unexpectedly bluesy performance, with slide guitar from Ronson and backing vocals from Dana Gillespie. The song was originally featured on the Ron Davies solo album *Silent Songs Through The Land* (1971). As far as can be ascertained, Bowie never performed the song again.

LADY STARDUST

Excellent piano accompaniment sets the tone on a piece originally titled 'He Was Alright (The Band Was All Together)' based on a line from the song. Most believe the 'Lady Stardust' in question was actually the queen of glitter, Marc Bolan, and when the song was performed on stage, just in case anyone missed the point, a picture of Bolan was projected on to a screen. It's really a rather touching, almost wistful, tribute to a friend, sung with affecting simplicity. "He was awful nice, really quite out of sight" sings Bowie as he describes the reaction of audiences to the young performer, and is bemused when they ask if he knows his name.

STAR

A Bowie boogie which tells how "Tony went to fight in Belfast, Rudi stayed at home to starve. I could make it all worthwhile as a rock 'n' roll star." Here Bowie imagines himself as a kid in the audience musing on his options. While on a higher level he could make a transformation into a star he could also "do with the money". The central theme of the album was thus rammed home with one of the album's better and more direct lyrics. This was one of four songs in which the word 'star' appears ('Starman', 'Lady Stardust', 'Star', and

Ziggy Stardust'). 'Star' wasn't actually performed during the Ziggy tours of the early Seventies but cropped up later on the album Stage as the last track on side one. In 1983 it was used during the 'Serious Moonlight' Tour as part of a nostalgic medley.

HANG ON TO YOURSELF

"One two!" Ziggy anticipates the audible count-in loved by The Ramones and latter-day punk bands. In fact this sounds like a punk rock band four years ahead of time. There are also overtones of Eddie Cochran's 'Summertime Blues', a record that both Bolan and Bowie loved to play as an example of *le vrai* rock 'n' roll. "We're the Spiders From Mars" is the cry during the hand-clapping finale of a high-speed rave-up.

One of the most convincing and entertaining performances on the album in terms of gay abandonment, it contained newly written verses and was a marked improvement on the original Arnold Corns version.

Bowie's acoustic guitar playing is well to the fore, complemented by a nifty bit of slide guitar work from Ronson. This ode to a predatory groupie and rock 'n' roll excess proved an ideal show opener through the 1973/74 touring season.

ZIGGY STARDUST

There was almost panic in the streets when this song was first unveiled. Certainly there was a commotion in the offices of the weekly music press as critics crouched over their mono Dansette record players and desperately tried to work out what it all meant. Hot debates raged on how Bowie was creating history by the second, pumping out new sounds, ideas and images in the white heat of creativity. It wasn't so much a problem this time with enigmatic lyrics as the feeling that the singer was taking pop music into a new and more fascinating dimension. The very tone of his voice, slightly manic and cat-like in its delivery, was enough to make fur fly, hackles rise and tempers flare. There was no doubt that, along with 'Starman', this was one of the stand-out performances by the Spiders, with Mick Ronson carefully plucking the notes and chords of a wonderful guitar introduction, practically a theme in itself. "Ziggy played guitar… " intones Bowie in one of the most memorable and often-repeated opening lines to any pop song of the era. There was a lot more to come. "Like some cat from Japan, he could lick 'em by smiling", and "Making love with his ego, Ziggy sucked up into his mind like a leper messiah". Here at last were clues to Ziggy's identity in this crucial track devoted to the being who summed up all the elements of Bowie's idea of a perfect pop star. At least we knew that, like Jimi Hendrix, he played the guitar left-handed and like Mick Jagger he had "God-given ass". In the final moments he sings prophetically "When the kids had killed the man I had to break up the band." Which of course was exactly what he did once Ziggy mania took too strong a hold on the teenage population.

SUFFRAGETTE CITY

One of the last two tracks specifically recorded for the album, 'Suffragette City' takes on board Bowie's growing awareness of the feminist movement that was gathering momentum at that time. Or at least that's the theory. It sounds more likely that he was just trying to avoid the clutches of a particularly heavy groupie. "This mellow-thighed chick just put my spine out of place." As a rock 'n' roll rave-up it provides a bit of light relief from the Ziggy doomscape. The saxophone backing is actually the sound of an ARP synthesizer played, sax-style, by Mick Ronson. During a break in boogie piano riffs Bowie lets rip with the cry "Wham Bam Thank You Ma'am". This came, not from the Small Faces, but from the Charles Mingus tune featured on his outrageous album *Oh Yeah*, played to death by blues and jazz fans on its release in 1962, who devoured such tracks as 'Eat That Chicken' and 'Oh Lord Don't Let Them Drop That Atomic Bomb On Me'. According to Mingus, drummer Max Roach frequently used the phrase "Wham Bam Thank You Ma'am" when he was "unable to express his inner feelings". Bowie fans however deduced that the phrase had some sort of sexual connotation. 'Suffragette City' was found on the B-side of 'Starman' when it was released as a single in April, 1972. Always a popular track – particularly on jukeboxes – it popped up again as an A-side coupled with 'Stay' in July, 1976. It was released around the time of the hugely popular *Changesonebowie* compilation album, but singularly failed to dent the charts in its own right. Nevertheless the song remained a part of Bowie's live set for many years.

ROCK 'N' ROLL SUICIDE

This dramatic opus wrapped up the saga of Ziggy as his five years of earthly freedom came to an end. It was the perfect number to conclude the live shows and was still being revived for Bowie's world tour of 1978. Released by RCA as a single some years after the album, it got to umber 22 in the UK charts in May, 1974. Says Bowie: "At this point I had a passion for the idea of the rock star as meteor. And it was the whole idea of The Who's line: 'Hope I die before I get old'. At that youthful age you cannot believe that you'll lose the ability to be this enthusiastic and all-knowing about the world, life and experience. You think you've probably discovered all the secrets to life. 'Rock 'n' Roll Suicide' was a declaration of the end of the effect of being young."

In a wonderfully dramatic and overblown performance Bowie's voice rings out "You're not alone... you're wonderful", the ultimate piece of group therapy, which hopefully, prevented any impressionable young fans taking his earlier words "you're a rock 'n' roll suicide" too literally.

"HOPE I DIE BEFORE I GET OLD!" THE WHO IN ACTION.

ALADDIN SANE

Released	April 13, 1973
Produced by	Ken Scott & David Bowie
Recorded at	Trident Studios, London
Musicians	David Bowie (vocals, guitar)
	Mick Garson (piano)
	Ken Fordham (saxophones and flutes)
	Trevor Bolder (bass)
	Mick Woodmansey (drums)
	Juanita 'Honey' Franklin, Linda Lewis,
	Mac Cormack (backing vocals)

WATCH THAT MAN

ALADDIN SANE (1913-1938-197?)

DRIVE-IN SATURDAY

PANIC IN DETROIT

CRACKED ACTOR TIME

THE PRETTIEST STAR

LET'S SPEND THE NIGHT TOGETHER (JAGGER/RICHARDS)

THE JEAN GENIE

LADY GRINNING SOUL

"I FEEL FOR ZIGGY TOO," CLAIMED BOWIE.

Ziggy Stardust was a hard act to follow. *Aladdin Sane* had an outstanding cover, depicting a striped Bowie, eyes closed with a crimson lightning flash famously streaking across his beautiful, vulnerable face. The image was strong, but the critics were unconvinced, accusing the album of having more flash than substance.

Apart from 'The Jean Genie' and 'Drive In Saturday', most of the songs lacked chart impact and the album lacked a strong concept, despite its bold title. Where Mick Ronson's guitar had once dominated, there seemed greater emphasis on the idiosyncratic improvisational skills of the band's new pianist, Mike Garson. Even so, amidst the ongoing excitement created by the Bowie PR machine and the sheer presence of the star himself, any new Bowie album was going to be hot news. It remained to be seen how many of the singer's young girl fans would be able to cope with increasingly off-the-wall performances: they may have found more comprehensible musical fare from Marc Bolan and T Rex. Indeed, given the bizarre mix of theatricality, free jazz, blues, rock and paranoia present in so much of Bowie's work, it was something of a miracle that Bowiemania took such a hold on a pop-hungry public during the early Seventies.

The answer lay in the shock value of his deliberately-contrived star image, spiced with a brace of tracks that were, in the final analysis, true pop classics. Many critics now see *Aladdin Sane* as Bowie's definitive statement on Glam Rock and as a celebration of decadence. Yet even his most ardent fans have expressed some disappointment with what they deemed a rushed project that had been erratically executed.

From 1972–73 Bowie was not only in the headlines, he was omnipresent in a compliant rock scene where he set the pace and prodded many of his fellow artists into action. Somehow, he managed to fit in his own tours and recording sessions into a tight schedule as well as busying himself with many diverse projects. He re-launched ailing rock band Mott The Hoople, producing their album *All The Young Dudes* and giving them the eponymously titled smash hit single that got to Number 3 in the UK charts in August, 1972. He also produced his pal Lou Reed's *Transformer* album (giving him an unexpected hit single – 'Walk On The Wild Side' – in the process) and worked on Iggy Pop and The Stooges' *Raw Power*. Never mind if Mick Ronson described the Reed sessions as "a bloody shambles" – Iggy Pop later disowned the album. It was all testament to the power of Bowie's magic that so many wanted to hitch a ride with the star.

Indeed, it began to look as if Bowie was rushing blindly ahead, doing too much all at once and not concentrating sufficiently on his own work. He admitted as much when he had time to pause and reflect: "When you get caught up in that wave of euphoria and become well-known, you are sure it's only going to last for a limited amount of time. So you cram as much work into it as possible. I was also writing and working up ideas for future shows before it all suddenly disappeared."

Bowie's new album was originally going to be called *A Land Insane*. He also toyed with *A Lad In Vein* and *Love Aladdin Vein* before settling on *Aladdin Sane*. "Originally I felt *Love Aladdin Vein* was right, then I thought maybe I shouldn't write it off so easily so I changed it."

The new music reflected Bowie's moods and feelings as he became sucked into an exhausting rock 'n' roll circus during his first year of heavy American touring. The camp-but-comfortable world of the London theatrical scene was superseded by the hippie freaks and aggressive groupies of New York and Los Angeles – an altogether different kettle of pills, potions and pot heads.

Even more disturbing and alarming was the way audiences came to regard Bowie as "the next great rock star" and began slavishly to emulate his look in the ultimate act of hero worship – at every show Ziggy and subsequently Aladdin look-alikes would turn up in droves. In the eyes of the fans, Ziggy was Bowie and Bowie was Ziggy. It was turning into a real life *Rocky Horror Show* writ large; harmless and flattering it might have been, but as Bowie looked down from the stage all he could see was a sea of clones and it was an unnerving experience.

**GROOVY BOOTS:
BOWIE ON STAGE.**

The effects on the lad from Beckenham were incalculable and lasted for several years. As Bowie commented later: "People treated me as they would have treated Ziggy. I became convinced I was the next Messiah. I fell for Ziggy too. It was quite easy to become obsessed night and day with the character. I became Ziggy, and Bowie went out of the window. Everyone was convincing me I was the Messiah, especially on that first American tour. I got hopelessly lost in the fantasy. The concerts got enormously frightening.

"Ziggy was created out of a certain arrogance, but I was young and full of life and it seemed like a very positive artistic statement. I thought that it was a beautiful piece of art, but Ziggy wouldn't leave me alone for years. That was when it all started to sour. It took me an awfully long time to level out. I really had doubts about my sanity."

With *Aladdin Sane* Bowie tried to encapsulate his American touring experiences in song and the results were certainly effective in that they reflected a wave of frenzied decadence and sheer physical strain. Bowie was part of the bubbling cauldron of madness heated by a boom in rock music that was bringing in money, fame and adulation, accompanied by a moral and physical breakdown among spectators and participants.

Bowie explained:" "'Aladdin' was really Ziggy in America. It was just me looking around and seeing what was in my head. It was the result of my paranoia with America at the time. I ran into a very strange type of paranoid person when I was doing Aladdin. I met some very mixed up people and I got very upset which resulted in Aladdin. I knew then that I didn't have very much more to say about rock 'n' roll."

Although Aladdin was a subconscious response to the new decadence, that was as far as it went in terms of structure. Indeed there was no particular order to the tunes, which were composed in different cities during his 1972 travels. Much of the writing was actually done on board the Greyhound bus that Bowie was using to get around the US, rather than undergo the trauma of a daily flight. The long bus rides meant that the concert dates had to be spread out, which enabled Bowie to concentrate on coming up with lyrics for the album and possibly to seek inspiration from the landscape rolling past the bus windows. "The numbers were not supposed to form a concept album, but there was a definite linkage from number to number. There was a special feeling on that album though, which I can't put my finger on." Although the critics were less than impressed, Bowie himself thought *Aladdin Sane* was one of the "most interesting" albums he had done so far.

Aladdin Sane was recorded at Trident Studios, London, with Ken Scott and Bowie sharing production credits. Once again the band included regular Spiders From Mars, Mick Ronson (guitar), Trevor Bolder (bass) and Woody Woodmansey (drums). This time they added the American pianist Mike Garson, Ken Fordham (saxes), and backup vocalists Juanita "Honey" Franklin, Linda Lewis and Mac Cormack. Bowie had hoped that Rick Wakeman would be their regular pianist but Wakeman was not available. An RCA employee recommended Mike Garson, a classically-trained musician and piano teacher. His audition, playing with The Spiders at the RCA studios, only lasted a few seconds. Mick Ronson told him he'd got the job and he was subsequently flown over to London from New York to finish *Aladdin Sane* at Trident. As well as becoming a great new musical force within the band he was also a Scientologist – a follower of the works of science fiction writer, the late L. Ron Hubbard – and had a great influence over fellow members of the band. Although Bowie resisted any religious overtures, he was delighted with the kind of classical overtures Garson contributed in the studio, as he made an immediate impact on such songs as 'Watch That Man'.

Sessions were completed by January, 1973, although Bowie had been playing concert dates in the US and the UK right up until December. Once he'd completed *Aladdin*, he had to rush back to America and the strain was such that he fainted on stage during a show at New York's Radio City Music Hall.

On April 6, 1973, 'Drive In Saturday' was released as a single, followed a week later by the album. Bowie fans were all agog. Duffy and Celia Philo designed the striking gatefold LP cover and Bowie's make-up was supplied by Pierre Laroche. It was claimed that the cost of devising such an elaborate cover (Bowie was sprayed in silver paint for the inside shot) was so high that the album had to be priced higher than average at £2.38! It didn't put anybody off. The album shot to the top of the charts and all Bowie's UK concerts were sell-outs. Strangely enough, not all of his American shows fared as well. In the mid-West, some of the venues were practically empty as only a few hundred tickets were sold. The androgynous Ziggy might have been all right for Hollywood and New York but it was plainly not for the folks of down-town Kansas City.

If touring had become stressful in America, back in England there was a good deal worse to come. Instead of what should have been a triumphant homecoming there was instead an ill-conceived show at one of London's biggest venues, the cavernous Earls Court exhibition hall, which had previously only been used for special events like the Motor Show. Although it would later became a regular rock venue, the first of two scheduled Bowie shows, held on May 12, 1973, proved to be a disaster. Nobody liked the vibes in the vast, impersonal building, the view of the stage was restricted and the acoustics were appalling.

A horde of visiting Australian yobs added to the ill-tempered atmosphere of the event, especially when they staged a mini-riot at the front of the stage. Some danced naked and urinated in the aisles and when they refused entreaties to behave themselves, Bowie threatened to call off the show. He left the stage visibly upset and only agreed to come back when the brawling had subsided. He subsequently cancelled the next show in disgust.

The debacle seemed to trigger a sea change in Bowie's attitude. Only three months after the release of *Aladdin Sane* came news of his shock "retirement". Bowie made the announcement to stunned fans at the end of his show at the Odeon Hammersmith, London on July 3, 1973. After a rousing performance during which guitarist Jeff Beck jammed on stage with Mick Ronson on 'Jean Genie', Bowie went to the microphone and spoke to the audience. He thanked the fans, the band and the road crew, then said: "Of all the shows on the tour this one will remain with us the longest because not only is it the last show of the tour but it's the last show we'll ever do." There were screams of "No!" from the stunned audience as the implications of Bowie's shock announcement sank in. He launched into a slow and emotional version of 'Rock 'n' Roll Suicide' with its haunting cry of "You're not alone... you're wonderful" that helped assuage the tears of the crowd. But it seemed that it was the end of Ziggy Stardust, not David Bowie. Even the group was taken by surprise. Apart from Mick Ronson, those Spiders who had recently been angling for a pay rise were kept in the dark about Bowie's true intentions. Yet the warning signs had been there from the start. They'd had The Rise; this was The Fall. "When the kids had killed the man I had to break up the band."

The Spiders From Mars performed once more – on Bowie's next album *Pin Ups*. When Bowie finally returned to live performance, he bid farewell to the Spiders, to Ziggy and Aladdin and to the extravagant makeup that had made him the leader of the ubiquitous Glam Rock movement that he had now so dramatically renounced.

WATCH THAT MAN

In the early Seventies, rock 'n' roll took on a deliberately sleazy and sloppy slant that was held to be hipper than the nervous high-energy style of the Fifties. The music of Bill Haley and Little Richard were already part of ancient history. If you were going to rock you did it like Little Feat, Dr John or the revamped Rolling Stones. As a result there was lots of "cling, cling, cling" piano beating, laid-back drumming and slide guitar playing prevalent among contemporary bands. This rapidly evolving style was called "buggy" (as opposed to "boogie"). You could "buggy" like this for hours, preferably with a cigarette pasted on the lower lip, and still expect a standing ovation from beer-can-toting fans in Stetson hats. This type of rockin' an' rollin' had its roots in New Orleans and pop musicians in need of a new musical fix appropriated it.

A similar brash garage-band groove permeates 'Watch That Man', and it is quite clear from this performance that the all-English Bowie had been heavily influenced by current American rock trends. Yet the song can also be compared to the well-established tradition of party songs with a strong narrative. A good example is Louis Jordan's 'Saturday Night Fish Fry', which is full of incident and characterization. Wanda Jackson's 1960 hit 'Let's Have A Party' also springs to mind, although the connection is rather more tenuous. Bowie's song relies heavily on words used for effect rather than any directly obvious message. What, for example, are we to make of "A Benny Goodman fan painted holes in his hands", beyond concluding this may be an oblique reference to Goodman's trumpeter Ziggy Elman, whose repertoire included a version of the popular tune 'Stardust'?

Nevertheless, this raucous and thoroughly enjoyable arrangement adequately describes Bowie's experiences at one of those notorious showbiz parties where the loosening of morals is discernible and high standards of public life are eroded. The party is thrown by one "Shakey", clearly a man suffering from some sort of nervous disorder if his nickname is any guide. Although Bowie is distracted by some of the other guests and pours scorn on their credentials, the Main Man, the guy who "talks like a jerk" but could "eat you with a fork and spoon", impresses him. Eventually, the lone Englishman finds the company and the vibes too overpowering and flees the scene. As the embodiment of claustrophobia and paranoia 'Watch That Man' becomes rather more than just an excuse for a rock 'n' roll rave-up. But it's that too.

ALADDIN SANE
(1913-1938-197?)

"Aladdin – where are you?" is the plaintive cry to be heard in stage productions of the famous pantomime based on the *Arabian Nights* and part of a theatrical tradition in Britain's folk memory. Even Cliff Richard has played Aladdin, relishing the role of the poor youth who obtains a magic lamp and ring, with which he summons genies who grant his wishes. Clearly the mythical character struck a chord with Bowie, once a poor youth and now a poor pop star (until he sorted out his business affairs). For magic lamp read Top 10 hit, or better still, renegotiated royalty agreements. Bowie's Aladdin is a much darker character than A Lad In Pantomime. Aladdin Sane sees a lad insane, concerned not so much with the prospects of a winter season at the London Palladium, as the imminent doom and destruction facing Mankind and Western Civilization. The dates in the title are significant. The first two, 1913 and 1938, are the years before the outbreak of World Wars I and II with an option on the long-awaited follow-up, which Bowie clearly expected at any time during the early Seventies.

Bowie explained at the time of the album's release that he was trying to preface the song with feelings of imminent catastrophe, a feeling that had begun to submerge him while trying to write material during his American tour. "It was the next jumping-off point for disaster." The insightful biographer, George Tremlett, has suggested that Bowie's inspiration here may have been Evelyn Waugh's novel *Vile Bodies*, which describes young people enjoying themselves with parties and champagne on the eve of the outbreak of war. Even so Bowie has been reluctant to be too specific about his influences – keep 'em guessing is always the watchword of the successful artiste.

"I don't think Aladdin was as clear cut and defined a character as Ziggy," says Bowie. "Ziggy was meant to be well defined with areas for interplay whereas Aladdin was pretty ephemeral. He was also a situation as opposed to just being an individual personality."

The Lad himself sings the piece, creating an icy tension as he attempts to contain an outbreak of impending violence by sheer willpower. It is left to Mike Garson to supply the manic physical outbursts, attacking his piano in a manner that suggests Keith Jarrett meeting Stan Kenton on a stormy night in Birdland. These fellow keyboard players (and band leaders) also loved to blend a rhapsodic classical approach with elements of Swing and the avant garde, using dissonance to create dramatic effects. The piano is the dominant instrument here, as Garson creates a suitably surreal background before launching into a free jazz freak-out. It is a measure of Bowie's confidence in himself that he is prepared to be upstaged, however momentarily, in the interests of art, creativity and collective music-making.

DRIVE IN SATURDAY

When it was released as a single, this got to Number 3 in the UK charts in April, 1973, but it was miles from the Top 40 in America where, despite all his touring, Bowie still had a long way to go. It wasn't for want of trying. "This was one of my more commercial numbers," conceded Bowie later. It was written on the road between Seattle and Phoenix and was inspired by the composer seeing a row of mysterious early warning radar type domes. He began to imagine a post-nuclear situation, after a war or radiation leak. In this grim new world, set in the year 2033, people's bodily functions and organs are so badly affected by deadly rays they no longer have a sex life, and have to watch movies at the drive-in to learn how to make love again. "Perhaps the strange ones in the dome can lend us a book we can read up alone and try to get it on." The sterile teenagers gaze at videos of their heroes and yearn for the good old days of unbridled sex. Bowie tells the story with due emphasis on key words and phrases "His name was always Buddy..." He sings like a tortured doo wop singer, a style subsequently adopted by fellow artists Ian Hunter, Steve Harley and Elvis Costello. 'Drive In Saturday' was unveiled at a gig in Miami in November, slotting neatly into the existing "Ziggy" show.

"I DON'T THINK ALADDIN WAS AS CLEAR CUT AND DEFINED A CHARACTER AS ZIGGY."
DAVID BOWIE

PANIC IN DETROIT

Bowie wrote this in Los Angeles after a night out with Iggy Pop, who had been busy regaling Bowie with lurid stories about life in his home town of Detroit. The city that is the centre of US motor manufacturing has been called the murder capital of America, a label which it has since taken steps to discourage in the interests of civic pride and progress. However, such was the impact of Iggy's tales of street violence that Bowie began to see the singer as a kind of urban Che Guevara, a political radical who kept his gun handy and drove a diesel van, the sole survivor of the National People's Gang. Here Bowie becomes more of a spectator, distancing himself from his own situation and perhaps revealing that his own descent into decadence is merely the result of disillusionment and the reaction to the disappearing prospects for the hippie or social revolution he once warmly supported. There is a scene where armed police wreak deadly revenge on the revolutionaries and Bowie sings "A trickle of strangers were all that were left alive." In the third chorus of the song the emphasis changes and Bowie reverts to being a schoolboy who finds his teacher "crouching in his overalls" and thus becoming, in Bowie's scornful eyes, a mere Establishment figure. Bowie then emits a scream and smashes his "favourite slot machine", which can be seen as a symbolic gesture – a blow against materialism. Then, racing ahead in time once more, Bowie scores "a trillion dollars" himself and becomes part of the materialistic capitalist system. The lesson is clear: revolutions are doomed. A sturdy Bo Diddley beat sustains a suitable air of panic and menace while Mick Ronson cooks a soulful guitar stew and the wordless background vocals whoop and shriek in a manner that has since become essential to the success of many Nineties dance hits.

CRACKED ACTOR

Composed during a stay at the plush Beverley Hills Hotel, this was conceived largely as a commentary on the exotic blend of personalities Bowie had spied from the safety of his limo while being driven down Hollywood Boulevard. "Suck baby suck" he declaims, imagining himself thrust forward into a future where he has become a 50-year-old film legend. Now on hard times, the man of the future is just trying to make a living, or at least indulge his pleasure, by embarking on more of those bizarre sexual practices that are such a recurring feature of everyday life within the Aladdin Sane family. In the world of the cracked actor, sleazy sex has replaced true love and become the yardstick of reality. The piece is performed with suitably raunchy harmonica wailing and some of Ronson's most bluesy guitar work.

TIME

'Time' is a robust piece of cabaret in which Bowie adopts a kind of Marlene Dietrich pose, except it is highly unlikely that Marlene would have used the word "wanking" in the text of such a performance. Quite how Bowie got this past the Lord Chamberlain, the Watch Committee and the League for the Suppression of Public Filth is uncertain but he boldly describes how "He flexes like a whore, falls wanking to the floor". I remember Bowie performing 'Time' at a special performance at London's Marquee club and seeing the look of shocked amusement come across a celebrated lady rock journalist as he first recited this pithy phrase.

Mike Garson bustles to the foreground, as Bowie becomes overwrought and crazed, a sorry spectacle for those who still remembered that nice young lad who sang 'Uncle Arthur' and 'Rubber Band'. "We should be on by now," he declaims, rather like the ventriloquist waiting for the jugglers to finish their act. There is much food for thought on what is an otherwise serious look at the fate of Mankind facing the ravages of time and its pitiless progress. Along the way he mentions "Billy Dolls" a reference to Billy Murcia, the drummer with the New York Dolls, who died in London in November, 1972, another of Bowie's celebrity friends who had become a victim of the Grim Reaper.

Although superficially a rather camp and theatrical performance, 'Time' does have a curiously hypnotic appeal and, as with even the most unpromising Bowie material, it repays closer attention and repeated plays as subtle nuances and hidden meanings reveal themselves to the assiduous listener. A pause for deep breathing is just one rather daring technical innovation by the singer and the leisurely but relentless pace has the drummer abandoning superfluous fill-ins for a welcome and highly efficient solid beat. Garson concludes a long-drawn jam with a memorable "plink" on his piano while Ronson contributes some deliberately grotesque howls that would make Jeff Beck's whammy bar fall clanking to the floor.

THE PRETTIEST STAR

The first version of this song appeared as a single released in March, 1970, with Marc Bolan on guitar, together with other members of The Hype, Mick Ronson and Woody Woodmansey and with guest, Rick Wakeman, on keyboards. Ostensibly about Bowie's girlfriend and future wife Angie and not, as many thought, about Bolan, the original single was a flop and withdrawn soon after release. The new album version, sans Bolan, has a sort of turgid doo wop feel about the vocal delivery, backed by some notably leaden and tuneless saxophone playing. Easily misheard in the mix, the opening lines sound like Bowie is proffering an advertisement for real coal fires, but the line is actually "Cold fire, you've got everything but cold fire." Bowie explains how he and his love, "the Prettiest star", will rise up all the way together and achieve great things, which was after all, their master plan for the future. Angela would help

MARC BOLAN – OH!
YOU PRETTY THING.

Bowie become a star and vice versa. Every concept album needs an intermission number during which the listener can make a cup of tea or fill in a crossword puzzle – this is it.

LET'S SPEND THE NIGHT TOGETHER

Jollity! Mirth! All the very attributes considered lacking in a superstar are revealed on this straightforward version of the Rolling Stones' hit from January, 1967. Here Bowie pays lusty tribute to Mick Jagger, the first androgynous rock star, and to his partner Keith Richards. These two were the Bowie and Ronson of their time, and remain so to this day. The performance ends with Bowie's spoken suggestion "Let's make love". This was clearly the object of his scheme to spend a night together with a partner. The Spiders are obviously having fun on a performance that blows away the angst and confusion of *Aladdin Sane* and Bowie himself seems to be saying "this is what it's all about", in a dry run for his next project *Pin Ups*.

Such is the success of this performance that many have uttered the heresy that the Spiders' version of 'Let's Spend The Night Together' is superior to the original. At this time Jagger and Bowie were hanging out together, drinking beer, shooting pool and just foolin' around.

THE JEAN GENIE

Undoubtedly one of Bowie's all-time greatest hits, this irresistible riff tune was written during an overnight stop in Nashville, early in the 1972 tour, and promptly recorded in the RCA studios in New York. The tune has all the stomping excitement of Sixties R&B. "On 'Jean Genie' I wanted to get the same sound the Stones had on their first album. I didn't get that near to it but it had a feel that I wanted, that Sixties thing," Bowie explains. Certainly this is one of the tightest band performances, with the section locking tightly together, Trevor Bolder's bouncy bass proving particularly effective. Bowie took just one day to write the track which emphasizes the benefits seeking inspiration while under pressure. In its construction and semi-spoken delivery it follows on from Bob Dylan's revival of traditional "talking blues" and can be seen as a kind of precursor all-pervasive rap style.

There have been conflicting theories about the model for the Jean Genie. Some simply look towards the Genie of Magic Lamp fame. Bowie has said it was all about Iggy Pop. "I'd just met Iggy. He was this character out of Detroit and I was trying to verbalize him in some way. I wanted to respond to the kind of image I had of him, which changed as I got to know him. But that's where that song came from."

The title is also a play on words, and some divined that this referred to homosexual French author Jean Genet. Bowie's 'Jean Genie' "lives on his back" and also "loves chimney stacks" which suggests the Genie either spent much of his time as an amateur chimney sweep or regularly indulged in strange and perverted practices. In real life, Jean Genet (1910-86) was an orphan and altar boy who turned to crime and spent many years in prison charged with theft

"ON 'JEAN GENIE' I WANTED TO GET THE SAME SOUND THE STONES HAD ON THEIR FIRST ALBUM."
DAVID BOWIE

BOWIE AND JAGGER WOULD PERFORM TOGETHER IN THE 1980S. 'LET'S SPEND THE NIGHT TOGETHER' WAS ORIGINALLY A HIT FOR THE STONES.

and prostitution. While serving a life sentence he began to write. His first novel, *Our Lady Of The Flowers*, caused a sensation, portraying a world of criminals and homosexuals scarred by violence, betrayal and death. Championed by French intellectuals, Genet was eventually granted a pardon and released from prison in 1948.

LADY GRINNING SOUL

A sensuous love song, 'Lady Grinning Soul' has the least contrived and most tasteful set of lyrics on an album otherwise noted for its sleaze. Garson's piano work is again heavily featured and he plays with the vainglorious rhapsodic style popular with saloon bar pianists of an earlier, more innocent age. While Garson is busy creating musical mayhem, Bowie warbles away with all the facility that marks him out as a remarkably gifted singer in the traditional sense. In an age when we have grown used to the gruntings of front men with no range, no pitch and no discernible vocal ability, it comes as a surprise to realize how much Bowie's gifts as a singer have been taken for granted. For when stripped of his "Ziggy" hairstyle and "Aladdin" war paint, he is a very fine singer and a consistently challenging wordsmith. If it sometimes appears that Bowie has come under too much scrutiny and has been subjected to too much criticism, that is only because he actually has something to offer that is worthy of debate.

'Lady Grinning Soul' gives an insight into a gentler, more human side of Bowie that reaches beyond the image and the need to shock. As with so much of Bowie's work he looks back into the romantic past as well as forward to an ominous future, always restlessly torn between realities and different perceptions of time. Amid the many contrivances of an extraordinarily provocative and diverse album, here is Bowie's soul stripped bare as he sings once more of breasts and caresses and strewn clothes; a sensuous paean of praise to the art of making love.

PIN UPS

Released	October 19, 1973
Produced by	Ken Scott and David Bowie
Recorded at	Chateau d'Herouville, France
Musicians	David Bowie, (vocals)
	Mick Ronson (guitar and piano)
	Mike Garson (piano and organ)
	Ken Fordham (baritone sax)
	Trevor Bolder (bass)
	Aynsley Dunbar (drums)

ROSALYN (DUNCAN/FARLEY)

HERE COMES THE NIGHT (BERT BERNS)

I WISH YOU WOULD (BILLY BOY ARNOLD)

SEE EMILY PLAY (SYD BARRETT)

EVERYTHING'S ALRIGHT
        (CROUCH/KONRAD/STAVELY/JAMES/KARLSON)

I CAN'T EXPLAIN (PETE TOWNSHEND)

FRIDAY ON MY MIND (YOUNG/VANDA)

SORROW (FELDMAN/GOLDSTEIN/GOTTEHRER)

DON'T BRING ME DOWN (JOHNNIE DEE)

SHAPES OF THINGS (SAMWELL SMITH/MCCARTY)

ANYWAY, ANYHOW, ANYWHERE (TOWNSHEND/DALTREY)

WHERE HAVE ALL THE GOOD TIMES GONE (RAY DAVIES)

By 1973, the previous decade already seemed like a golden age – when pop groups wore long hair and smart suits and R&B was all the rage. As usual, David Bowie caught the mood of the times when he launched into this unashamed wallow in the spirit of the swinging Sixties, just at a time when he was being heralded as the prophet of the new age of Glam Rock.

It was a great surprise, and even greater relief, when Bowie decided to fend off the urge to create yet another deadly serious, angst-ridden piece of rock art – at least for the moment. Ziggy Stardust was put on hold and Aladdin Sane could go quietly mad in a corner while Bowie learned how to smile and have fun again. He'd already pointed the way with 'Let's Spend The Night Together' on the previous album. Now he was ready to release an entire album of cover versions, loving recreations of some of the tunes made famous by his favourite groups. The Spiders were hot, Bowie was cool and now it was time to let the good times roll. And one of the elements that made this exercise so successful was the presence of guest drummer Aynsley Dunbar, chosen for the recordings in preference over Woody Woodmansey. With his powerfully dynamic playing style he made an immediate impact on the energy level of the Spiders, pushing both Bowie and Mick Ronson into a new dimension.

Bowie had already been booked for a mammoth 80-date US stadium tour but his label, RCA, wasn't willing to back such a risky project. They feared that whilst their star was potentially a major draw, as yet, he could not be guaranteed to sell out every show. Bowie was a media sensation but he was still a long way off conquering the all-important North American market. He still hadn't even secured a US Top Ten single. With company backing not forthcoming, Bowie solved the problem by proposing his retirement – hence the need for secrecy before his sudden announcement. Even his record company didn't know what was coming, let alone his backing musicians, the press or fans. Bowie's ploy ensured he had some breathing space. He could write new music, get a new band together and within a year he would be ready to play again. In the meantime he could have fun with *Pin Ups*. Far from committing rock 'n' roll suicide, his "shock retirement" was just about the best move he could have made.

The gods were smiling on Bowie. Instead of an unpromising stop-gap project, *Pin Ups* proved to be a highly-popular chart-topping smash hit. Even the cover was a hit. The picture of a frizzy-haired, bare-chested Bowie snuggled up with famous Sixties fashion icon Twiggy, set against a pale blue background, was a model of simplicity, and a testament to the work of photographer Justin DeVilleneuve. *Pin Ups* ranks with *Young Americans* and *Heroes* as one of the more charming and attractive of Bowie covers.

On July 8, 1973, a few days after the drama of the Odeon Hammersmith "retirement" concert, David and Angela Bowie left Haddon Hall, Beckenham to take the boat train to Paris. From there they went to a studio at the Chateau d'Herouville on the recommendation of Marc Bolan, who had been there recording his album *The Slider*. Elton John also favoured the studio, which he dubbed the "Honky Chateau", and it was later used by another keyboard-playing mate, Rick Wakeman.

On the *Pin Ups* sessions Bowie had intended to replace the Spiders with a more appropriate all-star backing group, but he couldn't get the particular musicians he wanted. However, Mick Ronson (guitar and piano), Mike Garson (piano and organ) and Ken Fordham (baritone sax) formed the nucleus of a very handy combo. Bowie had wanted ex-Cream bassist Jack Bruce, but Bruce was unavailable and so Trevor Bolder was called in for his last Spiders-related session and Aynsley Dunbar was firmly ensconced behind the drum kit. To complete the Sixties atmosphere, Bowie's old friend Lulu, who could out-sing most of the poseurs of the Glam Rock era just by drawing breath, was also on hand in the studio to supply good vibes. Bowie recorded her version of 'The Man Who Sold The World', released in January, 1974, which got to Number 3 – her biggest hit since 'Boom Bang-A-Bang' fiver years earlier.

On hastily-scribbled sleeve notes Bowie explained the plot behind his next album: "These songs are among my favourites from the 1964-1967 period of London. Most of the groups were playing the Ricky Tick, Scene club circuit (Marquee, Eel Pie Island la-la). Some are still with us."

The new Bowie album sounded just like a good night out at the Marquee. The band got its R&B rocks off and even though Bowie occasionally seemed to have his tongue firmly in his cheek, he sang as if he had reverted to being Davy Jones and his old band The King Bees and had finally made it to the top. Who needed Ziggy Stardust?

It didn't take a work of genius to recreate the old hits. Although Bowie had most of the 45s back home in Beckenham, he didn't take them with him to the Chateau. The guys knew most of the chord structures and Ronson, Garson and Dunbar worked up arrangements that either stayed true to the spirit of the originals or gave them an intriguing new spin. As Bowie recalled: "The Chateau d'Herouville was a lovely place to record an album. Warm, summer sunshine, a lovely chateau and a fantastic 16-track recording studio. It was enough to please any hardworking, city-weary young musician. We spent three wonderful weeks there recording all the songs which really meant a lot to me. The dinners were really momentous occasions with everyone seated at a super-long table with candles and dry wine, delicious food and all those

DAVID BOWIE: THE
ULTIMATE PIN UP.

beautiful faces with their sun-tanned cheeks and twinkling eyes. We recorded *Pin Ups* in one of two studios, the George Sand Studio, which was where the stables used to be."

When Bowie ventured out of the stone-built chateau it was to ride in a green Cadillac Fleetwood limo to The Malibu Club in Paris where he and his party could drink and dance until 4am. "Most nights however were spent in the studio where we'd drink French wine and record until dawn."

The Pretty Thing's best known number, 'Rosalyn', kicked off the album and provided a satisfying thunder of riffing guitars. The original had reached Number 41 in the UK charts in June, 1964. There was barely any let-up in the pace as one tune cut into another, as if a typical club manager was threatening to pull the boys off with a boat hook if they didn't finish their set on time.

Bert Berns' 'Here Comes The Night' was a hit for Van Morrison and Them in March, 1965, and Bowie unleashed a suitably soulful version, marred only by some out-of-tune saxophone playing. The Yardbirds' 'I Wish You Would' had Mick Ronson playing the insistent Billy Boy Arnold guitar riff that Eric Clapton had played back in 1965. But the biggest surprise was the band's

thunderous interpretation of Pink Floyd's 1967 Top Ten hit 'See Emily Play', with piano glissandos, wild synthesizer and menacingly deep vocals. Dunbar leapt into the fray on this Syd Barrett classic, giving the remaining Spiders a tremendous kick.

PINK FLOYD: PIONEERS OF UK PSYCHEDELIA.

Bowie sounded like a real pill-popping Mod on his sprightly version of The Mojos 'Everything's Alright', and The Who's mighty 'I Can't Explain' is taken with a cool, stealthy approach. 'Friday On My Mind', the classic working-man's lament, which shot Australia's Easybeats to Number 6 in the UK charts in November, 1966, suffered from a somewhat manic vocal. Here Bowie managed to sound like Sparks meets The Goons at a helium-gas inhaling party. 'Sorrow', the cover of the Mersey's song that got to Number 4 after its release in April, 1966, was a hit for Bowie too, when released as a single in October, 1973. Incredibly, this 'cover' did as well as 'Life On Mars?' when it peaked at Number 3 in the UK, only a matter of weeks after the reissued 1967 Bowie song, 'Laughing Gnome', had sold over 250,000 copies and got to Number 6!

Bowie brought out the laughing gas again for his interpretation of The Yardbirds' Number 5 hit 'Shapes Of Things', circa March, 1966. Bowie admired Keith Relf, the Yardbirds' lead singer, and even sported a similar blond fringe. Yet Keith never sang in the ludicrously over-the-top fashion that Bowie adopted for this tribute. It's actually very funny and anyone suffering from depression, angst, schizophrenia, or fear of radioactive mutants taking over the world, should listen to this and give way to peals of healthy laughter.

Bowie allowed himself a second bite at The Who with a block busting 'Anyway, Anyhow, Anywhere'. The drum work shows that if ever The Who needed a substitute, then Aynsley Dunbar was their man. Ray Davies' poignant Kinks' opus, 'Where Have All The Good Times Gone', was the perfect end to a thoroughly enjoyable set of performances, which makes you wonder why, years later, Bowie didn't form an all-British R&B group instead of Tin Machine, when he had the chance.

In August, when recording in France had been completed, Bowie and Angie rented a villa in Rome where he began working on his next idea, a stage musical based on George Orwell's chilling novel, *1984*.

They returned to London and Bowie cheered up his supporters by swiftly returning to live work, even if it was a TV recording session held at the Marquee Club in Wardour Street. Over three consecutive days, starting on October 18, 1973, he filmed a Midnight Special show for NBC, which included guests Marianne Faithfull and The Troggs. Bowie sang a new song '1984' as well as 'Space Oddity' and 'I Can't Explain' from *Pin Ups*, and he and Marianne sang a duet on 'I Got You Babe'. The show, which was only screened in America, saw the last-ever performance by Ronson and Bowie together, although Mike Garson continued working with Bowie for another two years.

When *Pin Ups* was released on October 19, 1973, it had advance orders of 150,000. It went to Number 1 and continued selling at the rate of 30,000 copies a week, eventually spending some five months on the charts. (When it was re-issued on CD in 1990 it included the bonus track 'Grown Up' by Bruce Springsteen, originally intended for a follow-up album of American cover versions, together with 'Port Of Amsterdam', the Jacques Brel song used on the B side of 'Sorrow'.) By the end of the year, RCA announced that David Bowie had sold over a million albums and a million singles in under two years of frenzied activity.

Pin Ups had achieved its aims and objects. It had defused tension, given Bowie a break and now he could get back to work on his next major project, *Diamond Dogs*. As Bowie explained: "The *Pin Ups* album was a pleasure. And I knew the band was over. It was a last farewell to them."

DIAMOND DOGS

Released	April 24, 1974
Produced by	David Bowie Released April 24, 1974
Recorded at	Olympic and Island Studios, London and Studio L Ludolf, Hilversum, Holland
Musicians	David Bowie (guitar, saxophones, Moog synthesizer, Mellotron)
	Mike Garson (keyboards)
	Herbie Flowers (bass)
	Aynsley Dunbar, Tony Newman (drums)
	Alan Parker (guitar)
	Tony Visconti (string arrangements)

FUTURE LEGEND
DIAMOND DOGS
SWEET THING
CANDIDATE
SWEET THING (REPRISE)
REBEL REBEL
ROCK V ROLL WITH ME
WE ARE THE DEAD
1984
BIG BROTHER
CHANT OF THE EVER CIRCLING SKELETAL FAMILY

GAZING DOWN ON
HUNGER CITY, BOWIE
UNLEASHES THE
DIAMOND DOGS.

David Bowie – half man, half dog. A strange but powerful image. After all, he could have been half man, half biscuit if the concept had been left to lesser mortals. The lurid cover painting of Bowie, by Guy Peelaert, made a striking introduction to his latest epic, the last in the trilogy that comprised Ziggy, Aladdin and now... the Diamond Dogs.

In which our hero rids himself of Spiders and attempts to make a record all by himself...

The album's doom-laden theme was originally going to be the basis of a full-scale musical, based on George Orwell's novel *1984*, with Bowie playing the lead role of Winston Smith. The book is a deeply disturbing and chilling depiction of a totalitarian state in a constant state of war, where citizens are ruled by Big Brother and the Thought Police, and kept under constant surveillance by CTV cameras found in every street and home. How unlike life in Britain in 2010. Orwell's vision was partly inspired by the bombed-out landscapes of post-war London in 1948, and by his own past experiences of media manipulation and police interrogation techniques. However, it came to be seen as a terrifying prediction of life in the future.

David Bowie was probably introduced to Orwell's book by a superb Fifties BBC TV adaptation, in which Peter Cushing played the rebellious Smith with a degree of sensitivity that only the brilliant and underrated Cushing could achieve. The play caused a sensation when it was first screened and left viewers with an unforgettably apocalyptic vision of the future. Throughout subsequent decades, people fearfully watched out for signs of Orwell's predictions coming true. One of the most astonishing revelations of the post Cold War period came when Russian politicians revealed that, although *1984* had been officially banned in the Soviet Union, it was secretly circulated in Government and KGB circles. Indeed, the ultimate, cynical irony is that it was used as a kind of handbook on how to run a totalitarian state.

When Bowie conceived the idea of setting 1984 to music he began blithely writing songs during a stay in the villa in Rome, using the rest period that followed the successful completion of *Pin Ups*. Unfortunately, when his scheme was drawn to the attention of the Orwell estate, his widow refused Bowie permission to base a musical on her husband's great work. Curiously enough, a decade later keyboard player Rick Wakeman composed an album (released in 1981) called *1984*, apparently without any great difficulties. If Bowie had succeeded in his aims he might have created the first stage rock opera. He was now left with a selection of songs without a home. So he decided to create his own vision of a hellish future called Hunger City, which became the basis of *Diamond Dogs*. In this post-nuclear-holocaust landscape, hordes of subhuman "Peoploids" roam about looting the shops among rabid dogs, themselves threatened by mutant rats. As it turned out, the songs were closer in spirit to the music of the Rolling Stones, T Rex or The Faces than the progressive rock of, say, King Crimson or ELP – bands that also dabbled in monstrous and threatening sci-fi images. Once again, Bowie used the superficiality of rock 'n' roll to provide a basis for deeper literary and artistic themes. He later insisted that there was no real intention to make the album a continuous dramatic narrative. That may have been more than he could cope with as a writer – any attempt to make a formalized structure would need to have been very successful indeed to avoid the strictures of the ever-present, circling packs of critics. Much was left to the listener's own interpretation, although the Orwellian motifs loomed large in such items as 'We Are The Dead', '1984', and 'Big Brother'.

Although sympathetic to Bowie's aims, many observers found *Diamond Dogs* bleak and pretentious. It is not even clear that Bowie himself very much liked the end product, generally expressing relief that, having taken on the mantle of producer, musician, composer, arranger and singer, he had managed to complete the work on time. It also gave him one of his best hit songs – the magnificent 'Rebel Rebel'. *Diamond Dogs* also provided the basis for one of the most daring, elaborate and statistically mind-boggling rock shows of the age, which finally established him as a superstar in America. All of this was going on while Bowie struggled to cope with the financial excesses of the rock business, the debilitation of an increasingly hedonistic personal lifestyle, and the problems of dealing with recalcitrant musicians.

91

"IT'S A PAINTING OF ME CHANGING INTO A DOG AND THEY'RE A BIT WORRIED THAT ITS COCK SHOWS."
DAVID BOWIE

During the latter half of 1973, Bowie took a well-earned rest. The first two months of 1974 were taken up recording *Diamond Dogs*. Sessions were held at Olympic and Island Studios, London and at Studio L in Hilversum, Holland. Old mate Tony Visconti returned to help out with string arrangements, while a team of session musicians was hastily assembled. They included both Tony Newman of the Jeff Beck Group, and the hero of *Pin Ups*, Aynsley Dunbar, on drums. Herbie Flowers replaced Trevor Bolder on bass and the dextrous Mike Garson was retained on keyboards. Bowie decided to dispense with the services of a guitarist and tried to play lead himself. The result was some of the most out-of-tune guitar work heard on record since Neil Innes unleashed his torturous solo on 'Canyons Of Your Mind' with the Bonzo Dog Doo Dah Band. The idea was, doubtless, to portray the sense of disorientation and fear engendered when ten thousand peoploids are being menaced by red-eyed, hungry mutants. You don't need a John Williams for this kind of close quarter street fighting stuff. Bowie certainly didn't need Mick Ronson.

Evidently, Bowie had been mightily miffed when Mainman management tried to launch the hapless Ronson as a rock superstar, with his own heavily-promoted solo album *Slaughter On Tenth Avenue*, just at a time when Bowie was battling to come up with a successor to *Aladdin* and *Ziggy*. Bowie needn't have worried. Although he put on a sell-out show at London's Rainbow Theatre, Ronson's album wasn't a hit, and neither was his debut solo single 'Love Me Tender', released by RCA in January, 1974.

Diamond Dogs caused a bit of a fright when it finally appeared in the shops. The half man, half dog creature on the gate-fold cover had its sex organs in full view. This was deemed offensive by RCA, which recalled the first batch of albums while the artwork was airbrushed and the offending bits judiciously removed. Those copies of the original vinyl album that reached the public became highly collectable. Early in 1974, when Bowie was asked about his forthcoming album, he explained that RCA was concerned about the cover. "It's a painting of me changing into a dog and they're a bit worried that its cock shows. But apart from the cock, everything's all right." Happily, when the album was reissued on Rykodisc CD in 1990, Guy Peelaert's artwork was fully restored. Two bonus tracks were also added to the CD: 'Dodo' from the 1973 Marquee TV recording session, and a demo version of 'Candidate', which had appeared in rewritten form on the vinyl LP.

Quite apart from panic at RCA, there was disquiet among some fans about the cover, with its fat semi-naked bitches grinning behind a doggy Bowie. Bowie may have had oddly canine teeth but this was getting ridiculous. The beautiful creature who once seemed so innocent even at his most decadent, was now reduced to a crude cartoon figure of fun. There were many who could not bear to look at the album, let alone play it more than once. Bowie admitted that he was one of them.

He said later: "I don't like a lot of my albums. A complete album... it would be hard for me to say I like. I like bits and pieces. A bit of it works exceedingly well and a lot of it only works. *Diamond Dogs* was not a concept album. It was a collection of things. And I didn't have a band. So that's where the tension came in. I couldn't believe I had finished it. I had done so much of it myself. It was frightening trying to make an album with no support and I was very much on my own. It was my most difficult album and it was a relief that it did so well. *Diamond Dogs* was a hard sort of album to live with at the time but it matured."

Despite misgivings among the critics (The cry "ten thousand peoploids" became a mocking catch-phrase) and despite its doomy theme, *Dogs* was a big seller and quickly went Gold.

In April, 1974, Bowie took the band to New York, where they spent two months rehearsing for a massive tour that Bowie intended to be the most spectacular in rock history. It also proved one of the most expensive. While he was there he spent a lot of time listening to black soul music at the Apollo Theatre in Harlem, which would influence the next stage of Bowie's career. Among the artists he raved over were The Temptations and Marvin Gaye, neither of whom featured much in the way of diamond dogs or mutant rats in their lyrics. It was as if Bowie was already yearning to be free of the straitjacket of "art rock".

Mainman bombarded the world's media with press releases announcing the tour and explained that it would feature music from the new album as well as Bowie favourites. "In simple terms *Diamond Dogs* is about the breakdown of an over-mechanized society. Bowie conceptualizes this vision of a future world with images of urban decadence and collapse. This theme will be extended into visual form for the stage."

The Diamond Dogs Revue finally opened at the Montreal Forum on June 14, 1974. The artist now known simply as "Bowie" put on a remarkable one-and-a-half-hour concert featuring 20 songs set in a heavily rehearsed and choreographed stage show. A specially-designed set – costing $200,000, conceived by Bowie and designed by Jules Fisher – was adorned with dancers, lighting effects and machinery that created the ambience of a Broadway show. The plan was to recreate Hunger City as a sort of decaying metropolis, and the mechanical props included a 20-foot-high bridge, which made a handy catwalk for Bowie as he sang 'Sweet Thing'. The bridge would rise and fall, while three lighting towers, designed to look like skyscrapers, beamed spotlights on to Bowie as he acted out the various characters in the story. He dispensed with his old Ziggy Stardust outfits and was clad in a light grey suit with red braces over a blue and white shirt.

The show opened with '1984' and featured 'Rebel Rebel', 'Moonage Daydream', 'Changes' along with 'All The Young Dudes', 'Watch That Man', and 'Drive In Saturday' – the only number on which Bowie would play guitar. When he sang 'Space Oddity', he appeared sitting on a 35-foot-long hydraulic boom projecting from one of the skyscraper lighting towers, spectacularly swinging him out more than 70 feet above the audience. In another carefully staged sequence he sang 'Panic In Detroit' wearing boxing gloves inside a boxing ring.

The show caused a sensation. When *Melody Maker* critic Chris Charlesworth saw *The Diamond Dogs* Revue in Toronto he reported: "David Bowie circa 1974 is not rock any more. He can only be described as an entertainer who looks further ahead than any other in rock and whose far-reaching imagination has created a combination of contemporary music and theatre that is several years ahead of its time."

The tour went to 28 more venues and ended at New York's Madison Square Garden on July 19, 1974, where the sound of barking dogs greeted the patrons as they arrived for each of two shows. During performances Bowie appeared to ignore the backing band and practically ignored the audience, as he tore through the barrage of songs. He often left without taking an encore – all done in the interests of preserving his mystique as the untouchable, remote, Garbo-esque star.

His backing group now included American lead guitarist Earl Slick, together with Herbie Flowers, Mike Garson and Tony Newman, all of whom had appeared on the album. It was a highly professional team, but the band threatened a strike at one point over their low rates of pay. Allegedly there was an altercation in the dressing room before a show that was due to be recorded at the Tower Theatre, Philadelphia on July 14 for the proposed *David Live* album. Understandably, the musicians wanted more money for recording. They weren't to know the shows were very expensive and overheads were high. They asked for more cash but were refused. As a result of the dispute, Bowie was in tears and it is said that chairs were thrown around the room before he eventually settled the matter himself. But it was a cause of further friction between himself and his management, for leaving him in this embarrassing position. After the first part of the tour had been concluded, Bowie swiftly found himself some new musicians.

There were also logistical problems to consider. Huge amounts of equipment had to be dismantled, moved from city to city and rebuilt. This proved a nightmare for the crew. It took up to 36 hours simply to build the set. On one occasion a truck arrived too late for a show which had to proceed without any effects. It was a hugely stressful time for Bowie and he must already have been thinking about moving on to something a little more manageable and easygoing. In August, during a break in touring, Bowie went to the Sigma Sound Studios in Philadelphia and began work on his next project, which he was planning to ensure was as far removed from a concept album as possible.

The American tour recommenced in September, 1974, with a week at the Los Angeles Universal Amphitheatre, but it was the end of the theatrical presentation of *The Diamond Dogs Revue* – it was too costly ever to be staged in Britain. Bowie continued touring the States with what was to become known as the *Soul Tour* instead.

"DAVID BOWIE CIRCA 1974 IS NOT ROCK ANY MORE. HE CAN ONLY BE DESCRIBED AS AN ENTERTAINER WHO LOOKS FURTHER AHEAD THAN ANY OTHER IN ROCK."

CHRIS CHARLESWORTH

Diamond Dogs was a bold gamble that partly worked, and was a step towards the new era of Bowie in which he seemed to see life more as a series of snapshots rather than as a linear progression. Bowie had been making use of American writer William Burroughs' well-known "cut up" method, moving bits of lyrics and themes around, which goes toward explaining the somewhat fragmented nature of the work. Musically speaking, he still had a lot to learn. There was some logic to using sleazy rock 'n' roll and pop soul as a background to higher literary aspirations, but the overall effect was a muddle of influences and half-formed ideas that was at once frustrating and provocative. It certainly didn't impress America's leading rock critic, Lester Bangs, who called it a "quasi-Orwellian concept album" full of "downright mediocre songs".

FUTURE LEGEND

The album opens with Bowie intoning a scene-setting introduction amid the sound of howling banshees. Civilization has broken down "And in the death ... the last few corpses lay rotting on the slimy thoroughfare," muses Bowie. He describes how red mutant eyes gaze down on Hunger City and goes on to talk about fleas who are the size of rats and his "peoploids" who are divided into small groups. They are apparently waiting for the year of the Diamond Dogs and they take it upon themselves to prey on the rich elite who they manage to spy on from the very top of Poacher's Hill.

On this track Bowie's voice is given a suitably weird treatment that sounds surprisingly similar to that of the decapitated robot in the movie *Alien*. To complete the surreal flavour, the band plays a sardonic version of the old Richard Rodgers standard 'Bewitched, Bothered and Bewildered' in the background. "This ain't rock 'n' roll... this is Genocide," shrieks Bowie. This ain't George Orwell either – the subsequent rock 'n' roll rave-up is more akin to Bobby Boris Pickett and the Crypt Kickers playing 'The Monster Mash'. The whole effect certainly led many to believe that perhaps Bowie wasn't taking this too seriously.

DIAMOND DOGS

The "Dowgs" (as Bowie pronounces the phrase in Jagger-ish drawl), are a threatening force for evil. The dreaded peoploids spend much of their time roaming the streets preying on the rich, who spend their time at wild parties where the guests no doubt include the gross-looking "boilers" who adorn the cover. Presumably, one of the major difficulties of coping with collapsed civilizations is the growth in the number of mutants and peoploids who start causing serious social and economic problems. There is reason to believe that the depiction of Hunger City was partly inspired by real-life stories that Bowie's father told him about his work for Dr Barnado's Children's Homes and the organization's origins among the impoverished orphans of Victorian London. Howls and groans greet a ramshackle performance that sounds like a series of T Rex riffs with a topping of cheesy saxophone licks. If this was presented today as a demo tape by an unknown band it would be hurled into a handy A&R office waste bin. Instead, back in June, 1974, it was released as a single coupled with 'Holy Holy' and got to Number 21 in the UK charts.

It has also been suggested that 'Diamond Dogs' was partially influenced by the writer Harlan Ellison, whose post-apocalyptic story *A Boy And His Dog* was later made into a film and expanded into a novel called *Blood's A Rover'*. Ellison's work was popular with a number of rock artists, among them Frank Zappa.

This raunchy rave-up also introduces the character of "Halloween Jack" to the song, who is "a real cool cat". "Ah ooh!" howls Bowie, doggy fashion.

SWEET THING/CANDIDATE/ SWEET THING (REPRISE)

These three items are linked together. Backward tapes herald Bowie's return to the world of sleaze that he knows best. "I'm scared and I'm lonely" he cries, adding "boys, boys, hope is a sweet thing". He reveals a surprisingly deep voice, before swooping into the higher register and then adopts a Hollywood movie accent for the line "I'm glad that you're older than me, it makes me feel important and free." Judy Garland rides again. Bowie contributes an intense guitar solo, still out of tune, but appropriate as the piece picks up and moves into Lou Reed mode. The three pieces segue into each other as the lyrics deal with low life, prostitution and drug-taking. "We'll buy some drugs and watch a band then jump in the river holding hands," he drones. In 'Sweet Thing' one of the longest pieces he had written since 'The Width Of A Circle', Bowie seems desperate to communicate and to nullify his ever-present sense of isolation. The message is that the only way to achieve a higher state is through love. 'Candidate' discusses the importance of sex as a tool for gaining power.

"I DON'T LIKE A LOT OF MY ALBUMS... LIKE BITS AND PIECES. A BIT OF IT WORKS EXCEEDINGLY WELL AND A LOT ONLY WORKS. DIAMOND DOGS WAS... A COLLECTION OF THINGS."
DAVID BOWIE

Sexual activity by does not give peace, pleasure or intellectual satisfaction – it is only a form of prowess by which others judge the participants. Although the combined pieces have some intriguing moments, unfortunately it all becomes a dreadful mess in the final moments of grinding guitar – a violent sound doubtless intended to offer a bitter commentary on the acceptance of decadence and excess over love and beauty.

REBEL REBEL

Hot tramp! Sudden relief from the dogs of doom – not to mention from the Bowie guitar. Here is a song about a raunchy tomboy rock chick who has torn her dress and whose face "is a mess". The theme owes much to Rolling Stones classics like 'This Could Be The Last Time' and 'Satisfaction'. The celebrated line "She's not sure if you're a boy or a girl" led some astute observers to deduce it might have been inspired by a Wayne County song called 'Queenage Baby'. It was commonly thought that Bowie himself played the tremendously funky riff that makes the tune a huge hit and is now hailed as one of the all-time-great rock guitar grooves. Yet there is a decidedly different sound about the whole track. It's as if it were recorded by another band in a different studio. It was revealed by Christopher Sandford, in his probing investigation of Bowie called *Loving The Alien* (Da Capo 1998), that the famous riff was actually played by a session guitarist. It seems that Alan Parker, who had previously played with Scott Walker, was invited along to Olympic Studios in Barnes to help record the tune. After being shown the chords by Bowie on an acoustic guitar, Parker played it back on electric guitar and did it again on tape. 'Rebel Rebel' was born. Although not a US Top 40 hit, it got to Number 5 in the UK after being released as a single coupled with 'Queen Bitch'.

ROCK 'N' ROLL WITH ME

A piece which owes much to the laid-back gospel feel adopted by Bob Dylan's backing group The Band, with Bowie singing more like a Cut Glass Cat than a Diamond Dog, helped along by some salty electric piano. On this tumbleweed epic Bowie seems to acknowledge that he has to stop using his stardom as an escape route from the real world, something that in real life he found very hard to do. Garson's Garth-Hudson style Hammond organ adds greatly to the mood of soulful redemption.

WE ARE THE DEAD

We are the dead" is the phrase intoned by Winston Smith and his great love, Julia, before a voice from a hidden telescreen chills their blood with the mimicking "You are the dead". It is one of the great heart-stopping moments in Orwell's novel. From now on Smith must give up his sexual affair and swear his allegiance to Big Brother and The Party. In his musical vignette, Bowie sings with rather more sincerity and less gimmicks than had become usual in this stage of his career. His series of semi-spoken verses, over a descending series of chords, is quite effective as he identifies with the grim fate of the hero. The track would later appear on the B-side of the single 'TVC 15', released in 1976.

1984

George Orwell (who died in London in 1950) would perhaps have been amused by this rather jolly theme, heavily influenced by the sound of Isaac

Hayes' disco theme from the 1971 hit movie *Shaft*. Orwell (whose real name was Eric Blair) had predicted a Ministry of Peace (that dealt with war) and a Ministry Of Truth that dealt with propaganda. He hadn't imagined a Ministry of Music that would have dealt with sampling and the synthesizer. Orwell's heavies might have found these devices of great use in the interrogation of prisoners.

The track '1984' is intended to explain Bowie's belief that the kind of rock decadence that had begun to engulf his life over the previous few years was actually propelling society towards the fate that Orwell had predicted. If a man born in India in 1903 could have coped with the uproar of 1974 he might have been flattered by all the attention.

On a more practical note, this performance has good production values, showing how recording techniques, under Bowie's tutelage, were moving into the modern era.

Surprisingly, given the song's context within the album, Tina Turner covered the tune to good effect on her 1984 album *Private Dancer.*

BIG BROTHER CHANT OF THE EVER CIRCLING SKELETAL FAMILY

"Two plus two makes five". That's what they say in the Ministry Of Truth, and if you don't love Big Brother it's Room 101 for you – that's the place where your worst nightmare resides. In Orwell's story, Winston Smith works at the grim Ministry building based in London, now the chief city of Airstrip One, third most populous province of Oceania, one of the world's three great powers. Amid the dismal landscape of a neglected city on which mysterious missiles occasionally crash down, the Proles and Party Members are kept under constant surveillance as the authorities check every action, word and thought. Their leader is Big Brother, whose image is depicted on huge posters bearing the legend "BIG BROTHER IS WATCHING YOU". Big Brother is all-powerful. You must learn to love Big Brother.

On 'Big Brother Chant Of The Ever Circling Skeletal Family', Bowie seems to pay homage to the idea of such a Superman. The piece moves into a chant and the repetitive tape loop phrase makes a rather contrived and inconclusive ending to an album that promises much but delivers a good deal less.

YOUNG AMERICANS

Released	March 1975
Produced by	Tony Visconti, David Bowie And Harry Maslin
Recorded at	Recorded at Sigma Sound Studios, Philadelphia and Electric Ladyland Studios, New York
Musicians	David Bowie (vocals, guitar, piano)
	Carlos Alomar, Earl Slick (guitar)
	David Sanborn (saxophone)
	Mike Garson (keyboards)
	Willie Weeks, Emir Kassan (bass)
	Andy Newmark, Dennis Davis (drums)
	Larry Washington (congas)
	Pablo Rosario, Ralph McDonald (percussion)
	John Lennon (vocals)
	Luther Vandross, Ava Cherry and Robin Clark, Anthony Hinton, Warren Peace, Diane Sumler, Jean Fineberg, Jean Millington (backing vocals)
	Tony Visconti (string arrangements)

YOUNG AMERICANS
WIN
FASCINATION
RIGHT SOMEBODY UP THERE LIKES ME
ACROSS THE UNIVERSE
CAN YOU HEAR ME
FAME

Stare into the eyes of the attractive, debonair young man on the cover of *Young Americans* and who do you see? His hair is neatly coiffured and backlit, giving him a shining halo of purity. Wrist bangles glint and smoke rises lazily from the cigarette held between delicate fingers. A smart check shirt reeks of normality. Is this androgynous Ziggy or alienated Aladdin? No, it's the boy next door, the sort of nice young chap any girl would like to bring home to Mum and Dad. The thought police at the Ministry of Love would have approved. This was the ultimate act of double think; Bowie ensured that the past had not merely been altered, it had been erased. Ziggy Stardust and the Diamond Dogs were no more. All hail the new Bowie.

"THAT PHOTO ON THE COVER ... IT LOOKS AS IF I'VE JUST STEPPED OUT OF THE GRAVE. HOW I FELT."

DAVID BOWIE

In retrospect it was not surprising that Bowie should have sought to make a sea change in his music and image, even before the Diamond Dogs had chased the last peoploid out of Hunger City. He'd reached the point where he'd drained all novelty from the guise of abnormality. In four years of frantic activity he had been anointed titular head of Glam Rock, hailed as master of the revels and dubbed leader of the rock 'n' roll pack. Madness and decadence could not be sustained forever; there came a point where normality seemed very attractive. The change in Bowie, epitomized by his appearance on the cover of *Young Americans*, with its classic photograph by Eric Stephen Jacobs, reflected the changes in his personal and professional life. It would have been tiresome and ridiculous to invent yet another wild and wacky character. He was getting older, audiences were changing and in any case *Diamond Dogs* had been difficult enough to sustain, and had already aroused a restless and suspicious response among his critics. He was still happy to keep the public guessing and, with *Young Americans*, he achieved a great deal on all fronts.

On a personal level, he was able to present himself as a mature artist and still retain his mystique and credibility. Given the huge impact created by his former alter egos, this was no easy task. And yet he was aided in some way by the changing moods of the record-buying public. His audience was growing up with him, and they welcomed the new look and the funky music. Bowie was letting everyone off the hook by taking off the mask and saying "Look, it's only me!"

Even so, he managed to retain his air of mystery. A clean-cut Bowie? Fine. But suddenly one wondered who exactly was this person we had been following for all those years, since the days of 'Space Oddity' and before? Who was this smart, clever young man who seemed to have no roots and no commitments, and who could reinvent himself at will?

In the past, Bowie had abruptly severed his connection with manager Ken Pitt and all those early blues bands. Now he sought to move on and break

101

free of entanglements, notably from his management company Mainman and from his wife Angie. He had already dispensed with Mick Ronson and the Spiders From Mars. Certainly the Diamond Dogs were due for the chop. So who was this iron man capable of such acts of defiance and manipulation? The real David Bowie lay hidden behind a defensive smokescreen. Somewhere there was still a nervous, nail-biting, chain-smoking youth imbued with over-riding ambition. He was defending his aims with that same flinty resolve that had ensured his initial success.

In 1974, Bowie decided that, even after all the records had been sold and the tours completed, he had to take charge of his own destiny. He still needed a helping hand to assist, advise and reassure, but a wiser, tougher Bowie would ensure that from now on he did things his way. There were still some errors of judgement, but ultimately the man who had caused such a sensation as a young dude survived, prospered and joined the ranks of the music world's financial elite. Bowie had once boasted he would be a millionaire by the time he reached the age of 30 – *Young Americans* was a stake in that glittering future.

David Live was the stop-gap album hastily issued between *Diamond Dogs* and *Young Americans* and released in October, 1974. One of the tracks, a rousing version of the 1966 Eddie Floyd hit, 'Knock On Wood', was culled from the double LP and released as a single in September, coupled with a version of 'Panic In Detroit'. Incredibly, this cover of an old hit did much better than 'Diamond Dogs' as a single and shot to Number 10 in the UK charts.

The album provided a veritable cornucopia of Bowie material (it included live versions of '1984', 'Rebel Rebel', 'Aladdin Sane', 'All The Young Dudes', 'Width Of A Circle', and 'Jean Genie'), yet there was something strangely flat about the sound. Although the cover was striking in its simplicity, showing as it did a cadaverous Bowie clad in a stylish blue suit with padded shoulders clutching a microphone, it all seemed somehow cold and lifeless.

Bowie went on to comment some time later: "*David Live* was the final death of Ziggy. God, that album. I've never played it. The tension it must contain must be like vampire's teeth coming down on you. And that photo on the cover, my God it looks as if I've just stepped out of the grave. That's how I felt. The record should have been called *David Bowie Is Alive And Well And Living Only In Theory*."

The album was rushed out by RCA to beat bootleggers who were already recording the gigs and churning out their own albums for the black market. *David Live* was a faithful enough documentary of the *Diamond Dogs* tour and showed how Bowie was rapidly moving towards the more relevant and contemporary "Philly" soul sound.

The *Diamond Dogs* tour took a break during the summer and then Bowie returned in order to complete the scheduled dates. The *Diamond Dogs* stage set was retained for this one show just for the benefit of a BBC TV film crew. By the time he returned in order to play some more US live dates in November, Bowie had slimmed down the stage set and concentrated more on playing soul-inspired music. His backing group was rejigged to reflect the new direction of his recent studio work, and now included Andy Newmark on drums, bassist Willie Weeks and ex-James Brown sideman, Carlos Alomar, on guitar. Luther Vandross, later a major star in his own right, was one of the backing singers. The tour that had begun as *Diamond Dogs* ended in December as the 'Philly Dog' or 'Soul' Tour.

Bowie previewed several songs from the forthcoming album on the tour, which wound up in Alabama on December 2, 1974. Understandably, after such an exhausting stint Bowie did not tour again until 1976.

During the summer of 1974 Bowie encountered his childhood hero, John Lennon, in Beverly Hills, at a party hosted by Bowie's actress pal, Elizabeth Taylor. Bowie and Lennon got on famously and Lennon even offered advice on how Bowie could get out of his management situation, drawing from his own experiences as an ex-Beatle. Lennon was fascinated by Bowie, whose "Ziggy" period he had missed during his years away from London. He agreed to meet Bowie again in New York and he even took an active role in the final hours of the *Young Americans* sessions. These began at Sigma Sound Studios in Philadelphia in August, 1974, with engineer Carl Parulow. At the start of the project Bowie had a less famous collaborator in mind – among those songs proposed for inclusion on the album were two Bruce Springsteen numbers: 'Growin' Up' and 'It's Hard To Be A Saint In New York City'. Springsteen was just an up-and-coming young singer/songwriter when Bowie spotted him performing at Max's Kansas City club, and was mightily impressed. As a result, Springsteen was invited to the sessions to hear his songs being given the Bowie treatment, but these were later dropped from the completed album. Another visitor at this time was manager Tony Defries, but in less constructive circumstances. He didn't like the new direction Bowie's music was taking, and, as a result, manager and artist had a row. It was the beginning of the end of their relationship.

After the tour dates were finished, in December, 1974, Bowie spent some time relaxing at his new home in Los Angeles. Then, in January, 1975, he went to New York and started further sessions at Electric Ladyland Studios, with engineer Eddie Kramer. While Bowie was in Greenwich Village, John Lennon called by and sang with him on two of the most satisfying and exhilarating tracks on the album: 'Across The Universe' and 'Fame'.

By this time Bowie had made drastic changes both to his show and to his backing group, which he now referred to as The Garson Band. Gone were the big sets and scenery from his shows and out went the old style rock 'n' roll approach in the studio. His most important collaborator was guitarist Carlos Alomar; great players such as Andy Newmark (drums) and Willy Weeks (bass) powered the rhythm section.

One listen to the new material on *Young Americans* indicates that a great burden had been lifted from Bowie's shoulders. Here at last were musicians who were consummate professionals, not just competent, but prepared to give the unequivocal support he needed as an interpretative, adventurous singer. They listened to each other, an attribute particularly noticeable in the rhythm section. Even wild man of the keyboards, Mike Garson, knuckled under and played for the team.

In interviews, Bowie explained just why he had made his latest changes and moved away from the idea of resorting to yet another Ziggy-like alter ego. "I think I always know when to stop doing something. It's when the enjoyment has gone. That's why I've changed so much. It's not a wise thing to keep on a successful streak if you're just duplicating all the time. That's why I tend to be erratic. It's not a matter of being indulgent. Everything I do I get bored with eventually. It's knowing where to stop. Doing a straight show is very exciting to me now. I couldn't imagine just doing the same show over and over again. It would be terribly boring. That's why I 'retired' the last time."

Most of the new material was written in the studio, and Bowie was sometimes rather disparaging when he reviewed this period in his life some years later. He called the results on *Young Americans* "plastic soul". But he allowed that it was good plastic soul: "It's not very complex but it's enjoyable to write. I did most of it in the studio and it didn't take very long, about 15 minutes a song. With *Young Americans* I thought I'd better make a hit album to cement myself in the States, so I went in and did it. It wasn't too hard really."

Just to check he was on the right track, he invited some of the fans who had been hanging out by the studio to come in and hear some of his new material: "We'd let them in to help out and give ideas… At night we'd go to clubs with them. We had a big end-of-recording party and they came to that and we played the album mixes."

Not long after he finished recording, Bowie began work on his first film, *The Man Who Fell To Earth*, which was shot in Mexico. From then on Bowie became an internationally-respected figure, and began the long trawl both to respectability and to financial security.

Young Americans was released on March 7, 1975. It came just as it was announced that Bowie had finally split with Mainman. In July, Bowie told the press: "Me and rock 'n' roll have parted company. Don't worry. I'll still make albums with love and fun, but my effect is finished. I'm very pleased. I think I've caused quite enough rumpus for someone who is not even convinced he's a good musician."

By now many fans were wondering whether the artist that Frank Sinatra apparently refused to meet, because he was "an English fag", had ever really been the supposed bisexual queen of Ziggy days. Even Bowie wasn't sure. "I suppose I do fancy blokes quite a lot, but I spend more time with chicks, particularly black chicks. The only type of chicks I can't stand are New York feminists. Get them into bed and after five minutes they want you to do something funny with a light bulb. It's all so academic."

Recorded in just eight all-night sessions, *Young Americans* has since been described as one of the most influential albums of the Seventies. It put the seal of approval on the burgeoning disco scene, hitherto the preserve of the underground club culture, and bid *adieu* to the restraints of conventional rock music.

The eventual CD version of the album came with three bonus tracks. These were 'Who Can I Be Now?', a soulful item accidentally left off the original album; 'It's Gonna Be Me', a soul ballad previously sung live on the 'Philly Dogs' Tour; and 'John I'm Only Dancing Again', a new version of the 1972 single with David Sanborn on alto sax.

YOUNG AMERICANS

A lilting samba rhythm pervades the title track that kicks off with a bouncy drum intro and some soulful Sanborn sax. Traces of Otis Redding and Curtis Mayfield are revealed in the breathless vocal style that Bowie adopts. A succession of gasps, sharp intakes of breath and high-note warbles gives the distinct impression that, as well as singing, David is undergoing some kind of physical activity – possibly on a trampoline. "Do you remember, your President Nixon... the bills you have to pay or even yesterday?" he asks in a rap-style delivery that grows increasingly urgent and indistinct.

When the single version of 'Young Americans' was released in February, 1975, coupled with 'Suffragette City', Bowie had already been singing this breathless, enthusiastic song on tour. It served to build up expectations for the album, which was held back while sales of *David Live* ran their course. Cut in one evening, the song epitomized the new Bowie that the world was waiting to hear, especially all those back home who hadn't been exposed to the 'Soul' Tour. It seems that nearly everyone was delighted with the clean-cut image as well as the disco groove. Bowie was pleased that he was rid of those mutant rats and pesky peoploids, and the fans were happy for him. There was a sigh of relief all round. The record was even a hit. A big one. It gave Bowie his first solid US chart placing since 'Space Oddity' – 'Young Americans' yanked away to Number 28 in the *Billboard* Top 40 in April, 1975. In the UK it peaked at Number 18.

The song had been inspired by Bowie's experience of the burgeoning disco and club scene that he'd found during visits to New York. Always on the ball when it came to detecting new trends, he realized that dance music was going to become bigger and more relevant than hard rock. It was

"... I'VE CAUSED QUITE ENOUGH RUMPUS FOR SOMEONE WHO IS NOT EVEN CONVINCED HE'S A GOOD MUSICIAN."

DAVID BOWIE

certainly a lot more fun. He explained: "Hanging around the clubs I began to feel the new disco thing. I just got caught up in the mood. 'Young Americans' was based on that, and I sort of crammed my whole American experience into the song and that's the way it came out."

It is supposedly about a young married couple who are not sure if they're still in love. In a way, it is also about whether Bowie himself was in love with the America he was still discovering. It's possible to hear references not only to President Nixon of Watergate scandal fame, but to the John Lennon line "I heard the news today – oh boy", from 'A Day In The Life', which is quoted by the busy backing vocalists. As Bowie explained: "The song is about a newly-wed couple who don't know if they really like each other. Well, they do, but they don't know if they do or don't. It's a bit of a predicament!"

WIN

A gentle, subtle ballad, Bowie sings this with uncharacteristic restraint, although he allows his voice to be given some kind of electronic, synthesized treatment. It neatly complements the ebb and flow of the rhythm and melody set up by the keyboards, sax and vocal chorus. The slow pace allows his words to wash over like the sea. "You've never seen me hanging naked and wired", he intones, pointing out that behind his celebrated image lies a real and vulnerable, flesh-and-blood human being. In fact, most of the population had seen him at least partially naked, thanks to a multitude of highly theatrical stage performances. Even so, Bowie felt this was a "get up off your backside" song with a strong moral message. "It was written about an impression left on me by people who don't work very hard or do anything much, or think very hard. To them it's easy, all you've got to do is win." Bowie aficionados felt this was one of his best tracks on the album because it seemed to represent the real David Bowie, hidden for so long behind the cracked actor.

FASCINATION

At one stage it was rumoured that "Fascination" would be the title of the album. (In fact the working title was 'One Damn Song'.) This attractive song was co-written with Luther Vandross, then one of Bowie's backing soul singers. It was based on a Vandross hit called 'Funky Music (Is A Part Of Me)'. Born in New York City in 1951, Vandross was a singer, songwriter and producer in his own right. He eventually enjoyed his first Top 40 hit with 'Never Too Much' in 1981 and got to Number 4 in the US with 'Power Of Love'/'Love Power' in 1991.

Bowie sings as if he'd been a soul boy all his life, with no hint of the glittery androgyne of yesteryear. As he intones the hookline the backing vocalists repeat the phrases over a light and springy beat. Carlos Alomar makes use of his wah wah pedal, creating layers of rhythm guitar to cushion Bowie's progress as he whips himself into a lather. With the introduction of the synthesizer and other studio effects, this was the dawn of the age when it was no longer possible to easily identify the sound sources on a record. The drumming remains surprisingly weak, but the original vinyl version of 'Fascination', re-mastered for the CD reissue, has a vastly improved sound.

RIGHT

An incredibly simplistic guitar riff creates the basis for the aptly-named 'Right'. Carlos chords away, altering the note from major to minor and back again while the girls chant "Never no turning back". It's basic, simple and hugely effective.

Bowie had a curious idea about the *raison d'etre* for this song: "'Right' is putting over a positive drone. People forget the sound of Man's instinct is a drone, a mantra. It reaches a particular vibration, not necessarily on a musical level." It was Bowie's fiendish plan to implant an erotic mantra into the psyche of all Mankind through music, and in the process extinguish man's tendency towards mindless violence. As an example of "blue eyed soul" recorded in the heart of Philadelphia, and of "Philly Sound" territory, mixed at the Record Plant in New York, this song is undoubtedly one of the album's high spots. It was among those new numbers regularly performed live along with 'Somebody Up There Likes Me', during the 'Philly Dogs' Tour.

SOMEBODY UP THERE LIKES ME

Here, Bowie tries to warn of the dangers of the cult of the personality and of the likelihood of another mad dictator attempting to corrupt the minds of the masses and seize power by appealing to their baser instincts. As he explained:

"This is a 'Watch out mate, Hitler's on his way back'. It's your rock 'n' roll sociological bit." The phrase comes from the title of a 1956 movie starring Paul Newman in the role of Rocky Graziano, a hoodlum and middleweight champion boxer. The tune rather plods along, and there is an excess of sub-Junior-Walker-style alto sax wailing. This was probably among those numbers that Bowie wrote and recorded at speed in the studio; it ended up as a rather confusing diatribe that hints at some of the political obsessions that, once they surfaced fully, would cause him grief.

ACROSS THE UNIVERSE

After the Philadelphia sessions at Sigma Sound, Bowie went to the Record Plant in New York to mix the sessions using a 24-track desk. The album was all but finished, yet he was still debating whether to add another track. He eventually decided to try cutting a version of one of his favourite John Lennon compositions 'Across The Universe'. The result was an intriguing new version of the song featured on the Beatles' 1970 album *Let It Be*. As Bowie later said: "This was a flower power sort of thing John Lennon wrote. I always thought it was fabulous but very watery in the original, and I hammered the hell out of it. Not many people like it. I like it a lot and I think I sing very well at the end." Some critics suggested that Bowie was somehow utilizing the presence of John Lennon, New York's most celebrated guest-resident, for his own nefarious purposes – they didn't know that Bowie and Lennon had become mates and simply enjoyed making music in a studio. Said Bowie: "People say I 'used' John Lennon on the track. But no one uses John Lennon. John just came and played on it. He was lovely." Bowie sings the line "Nothing's gonna change my world" with a strangely deep and gurgling tone, as if he is partially immersed in water. Later, as he becomes more frantic and neurotic, Bowie begins to sound like Sid Vicious of the Sex Pistols – a full year or more before that ensemble first charmed the world.

CAN YOU HEAR ME

Written with somebody specific in mind, at the time of the album's release Bowie wasn't keen on letting the world in on his secret. "That is a real love song," was all he would say. Long after he had finally split up with wife Angie, it was determined that the song was almost certainly aimed at new girlfriend Ava Cherry, who happened to be one of the backing vocalists on the team and whose solo singing career Bowie was keen to promote.

There is a strong Stax feel to this slow tempo ballad with strings and a rather eccentric vocal. Despite the nifty guitar fills, it's really rather dull. Only the unaccompanied vocal coda instills some interest into the proceedings. The use of falsetto pre-dates the Bee Gees, who began jive-talking a few months later. 'Can You Hear Me' was issued on the B-side of the 'Golden Years' single in November, 1975.

FAME

As is often the case with those obvious hit tracks that invariably appear on Bowie albums, this one was put on as an after-thought and came about as a particularly happy accident. 'Fame' was added to the original album tapes some time after the original Sigma sessions with Visconti had been completed and allegedly without his knowledge.

The result of a jam session at Electric Ladyland, 'Fame' has John Lennon once again providing inspiration and more than a touch of Beatle magic. The lyric consists of another mantra-like chant of the key word that serves as a kind of unspoken commentary on the condition that both men had endured for many years. "This was more or less sung about what we were both doing," said Bowie rather enigmatically in the aftermath of the sessions. It wasn't so much fame that bothered them, as music biz problems. They decided to write the song together in the wake of their shared experiences. Bowie explained: "With John Lennon it was more the influence of having him in the studio that helped. There's always a lot of adrenalin flowing when John is around, but his chief addition was the high-pitched singing of 'Fame'. The riff came from Carlos Alomar, and the melody and most of the lyrics came from me. But it wouldn't have happened if John hadn't been there. He was the energy and that's why he's got a credit for writing it; he was the inspiration."

It is believed that the original impetus for 'Fame' came from a number that The Garson Band had been playing on the last dates of the 'Philly Dogs' Tour. The boys had been working out on a 1961 tune by The Flares called 'Foot Stomping'. David Bowie recalled the circumstances: "The riff that Carlos had developed, I found fascinating." Bowie kept telling Alomar that it was a waste to do it on somebody else's song and that in fact they should use it on something of their own devising. "So we were playing that riff for

**"... IT WOULDN'T
HAVE HAPPENED
IF JOHN HADN'T
BEEN THERE"**

DAVID BOWIE (ON
JOHN LENNON)

John Lennon in the studio when he came down for the day and we said 'What do you make of this John?' He was playing along with it, just muttering to himself in a corner saying 'Aim... aim!' It just fell into place when he said 'Fame!'" Apparently Lennon then added some rhythm guitar and the backing track was put together in about 20 minutes. Bowie went away to complete the lyrics, and 'Fame' was finished.

An alternative version of events has it that when Lennon arrived at the Record Plant he picked up an acoustic guitar and began playing 'Shame, Shame, Shame', a 1975 Top 20 hit by Shirley And Company (a studio group that consisted of Shirley Goodman of Shirley and Lee, and Kenny Jeremiah of the Soul Survivors). Carlos Alomar picked up the riff, and when Bowie came into the studio he demanded to know what they were playing. Lennon told Bowie that making hit singles was dead easy – all you needed was a hook line, the right kind of feeling, and a solid back beat. Mightily encouraged, Bowie went off to write some lyrics and put the piece into classic rhythm and blues form. Taking various bits of the vocal, guitar and rhythm tracks, the whole lot was given the cut-up treatment, with sections of the master tape being run backwards and other effects brought into play. It all climaxed with the eerie vocal descent through a series of octaves that delighted everyone the first time they heard it. "What you get is no tomorrow... what you need you have to borrow," sang Bowie in an ill-concealed poke at his management.

Even today, when digital recording has transformed the sound of pop music, 'Fame' in its original format retains its hypnotic power and startling impact. The drums are way up front in the mix, tight and with only a choking hi-hat to break up the beat, Carlos Alomar's guitar is funk personified, and Bowie's tortured toying with the key phrase is darkly amusing.

In truth, there is hardly any comparison to be made between 'Fame' and the rest of the material on *Young Americans*, which is attractive and has its high points, but is essentially bland pop soul. 'Fame' rightly caused a sensation. RCA pressed up 250,000 singles and the edited version rocketed straight to Number 1 in the US chart in October, 1975. Back in the UK, however – echoing Lennon's own commercial fortunes at the time – 'Fame' only reached Number 17 in the charts. Some diehard Bowie/Ziggy fans clearly felt alienated by the new disco sound.

Bowie was later delighted when he heard that the great James Brown himself had been impressed enough with 'Fame' to cut a version of the song. For the boy from Beckenham who had spent so many years in the thrall of other musicians, this was the ultimate accolade.

STATION TO STATION

Released	January 1976.
Produced by	David Bowie And Harry Maslin
Recorded at	Cherokee Studios, Hollywood
Musicians	David Bowie (vocals)
	Carlos Alomar, Earl Slick (guitars)
	Roy Bittan (keyboards)
	George Murray (bass)
	Dennis Davis (drums)

STATION TO STATION
GOLDEN YEARS
WORD ON A WING
TVC15
STAY
WILD IS THE WIND

STARRING ROLE: BOWIE AS THOMAS NEWTON IN *THE MAN WHO FELL TO EARTH* (1975).

Fame brought mixed blessings to the boy who would be Bowie. Living in America from April 1974 to March 1976, he shifted artistically toward dance music but began a personal decline into rock 'n' roll hell. His debilitating battles on the managerial and matrimonial fronts took their toll on his health, mental state and sense of well-being. There were yet more changes – and not always for the better.

Adopting his latest persona, he became "the thin white duke", a rather cold, almost lifeless figure. After spending a large part of 1975 making his first major feature film, *The Man Who Fell To Earth*, Bowie took on many of the characteristics of the role he'd played with distinction – a common phenomenon that affects actors forced to delve too deeply into their roles. In playing the part of Thomas Jerome Newton, an alien from outer space who crashes to Earth in America, Bowie seemed to adopt alien attitudes himself. "I was Newton for six months," he confessed later.

His somewhat lofty and distant demeanour was exacerbated by his brief flirtation with the downside of the rock'n'roll lifestyle. He has referred to this period both in his songs and in interviews, and it was all part of a general malaise that seemed to affect the intelligent, but easily-influenced, poet.

Previously, Bowie had an older brother to lean on. In addition, he also had schoolfriends, girlfriends, as well as a manager who cared about him, and the kind of musical mates who really did have his best interests at heart. These were the loyal, good people back home. It meant that even when he was undergoing his wildest flights of fancy, he could always rely on them to bring him back to Earth. Now he was wandering alone in Gotham City, surrounded by the mixed-up and the dangerous. His head was filled with pseudo-religious, magical and half-baked political ideas, and he seemed to be increasingly vulnerable and stripped of that useful defence mechanism referred to as 'common sense'.

Cocaine had begun to flow freely throughout the music business during the early Seventies. This is no place to get into a long rap about causes and effects, but money, fame and drugs do seem to go rather well together. Clearly somebody was making a good living by parting rock stars from their royalties. So what? Wasn't that all part and parcel of the whole thing about being a rock 'n' roll rebel?

Unfortunately, the process left many of the victims stripped not only of their money, but of any chance of making hit records in the future. As the list of casualties grew, it left a roster of ill-tempered, confused, paranoid and unemployable former artists. David Bowie too had his dark periods but he never entirely lost his grip on reality. He had too much to offer, too much talent and, ultimately, too much respect for himself to end up on the rock 'n' roll scrap-heap.

In the Spring of 1975, David Bowie moved from New York to Los Angeles and rented a large house in Beverly Hills that was crammed full of Egyptian decor. It's interesting to note that he was once photographed as an Egyptian prince. Bowie gave an explanation of his choice of home decor: "I had this more-than-passing interest in Egyptology, mysticism, and the cabala. At the time it seemed transparently obvious what the answer to life was. My whole life would be transformed into this bizarre nihilistic fantasy world of impending doom, mythological characters and imminent totalitarianism."

Bowie was naturally interested in the more unusual strands to life and its mysteries, but he had never allowed this to dominate him in the past. Part of the problem now was the vast number of hangers-on who were attracted by the exotic star. In a way, he had to live up their expectations. And how were they to know that their start would probably prefer to spend the night in, watching old movies on TV, than indulging in orgies and endless partying? He confessed later: "I surrounded myself with people who indulged my ego. They treated me as though I was Ziggy Stardust, never realizing David Jones might be behind it. I was zonked out of my mind."

Old friends had warned Bowie that if he continued with the life he was leading in Los Angeles it was possible that he would not survive. He took heed, but only when it was nearly too late.

At first Bowie flung himself into the vortex at the start of a year which he was later to describe as being "a complete blank". Even so, he managed to fit in a lot of important business, including career moves and recording sessions. On the business side, in March of 1975, Bowie ended his dispute with Mainman. In the meantime he had also found himself a new manager, Los Angeles-based Michael Lippman. Their relationship was not destined to last long. Even so, it seemed that after all the business and personal upheavals it now looked pretty much as if David had finally put his affairs in order and as a result, a much brighter future lay before him.

In July and August, 1975, filming began for *The Man Who Fell To Earth*. It was a film directed by Nicholas Roeg that was to be shot on location in the USA, in the deserts around Lake Fenton, New Mexico. Bowie acquitted himself well at the task, and he was complimented on his professionalism. With proper tuition Bowie could perhaps even have been the Dirk Bogarde of his generation. As it was, he proved a more successful rock-star-turned-actor than Mick Jagger.

In September, 1975, immediately after filming of *The Man Who Fell To Earth* was complete, it was back to face the music for young David – a new album needed to be put together. For this one, Bowie headed for Cherokee Studios in Hollywood to begin recording sessions for what would become *Station To Station*. He used some of the musicians who had worked with him on *Young Americans* – Carlos Alomar, Earl Slick, on guitars, Dennis Davis on drums, George Murray on bass and guest star Roy Bittan from Bruce Springsteen's E Street Band on keyboards. Their material proved to be a strange mixture of both European and American influences. There was an early touch of Kraftwerk-style electronic surrealism, but most of the tracks reflected the current surge of Euro Techno Disco, only with a more cerebral lyrical content. Once again, the lines between Bowie the influence and Bowie the absorbent sponge became blurred.

Although there were only five original tunes scheduled for the album, it took two-and-a-half months of intensive studio work to write and record. It was made on a 24-track desk, which gave the producer and engineer scope for alterations. But Bowie made so many changes that the music eventually heard on the record was largely improvised on the spot. This belied the subsequent accusations of critics that too clinical an approach had been deployed.

The album was going to be called *The Golden Years* and was also referred to as *The Return Of The Thin White Duke* in deference to a key line in the opening cut. Bowie decided to work with Harry Maslin as his producer, who had previously worked with him on the 'Fame' session. Bowie and Harry worked by night and slept by day as the sessions progressed. "I hate sleep, I prefer staying up and working all the time," Bowie said. The band might have had other ideas, but they were expected to keep up the pace, sometimes playing or working on tracks for up to 46 hours at a stretch. During this intense period Bowie often went without food or drink, beyond the odd glass of milk. He grew thinner and thinner as he worked himself into the twin roles of ravaged rocker and mutated movie actor.

The somewhat scary Duke was one of Bowie's least popular characterizations. The successor to Ziggy, Aladdin and Diamond Dog, "The Thin White Duke" was meant to represent the man inside, the strange inner being who looks both coldly and disdainfully upon the warmth of natural human relationships. Indeed, the real Bowie had become less close to many old friends during this troubled period including Mick Ronson, Lou Reed and even the mighty Bob Dylan, who incidentally revealed that he wasn't a great fan of the *Young Americans* album.

Bowie began depicting himself as the lonely expatriate, the ducal Englishman yearning to return home to rediscover his roots. There were good reasons for his pressing need to get back to a semblance of normality. During his stay in Los Angeles it was rumoured that he had become increasingly involved in strange hobbies, but this was little more than exaggerated gossip.

As a city, Los Angeles was seething with alternative philosophies and occult practices that seemed destined to lure the unwary into a morbid mesh. What most people back home took to be the subject of a jolly good yarn by Dennis Wheatley, or a good plot for a new Hammer Horror film, was turned into a serious lifestyle by the denizens of Seventies LA.

Bowie was lonely, disorientated, under constant business pressures, facing the break-up of his marriage and, perhaps, not quite sure in which way to develop his musical career. Hardly surprising, then, that a shattered Bowie

"I SURROUNDED MYSELF WITH PEOPLE WHO INDULGED MY EGO. THEY TREATED ME AS THOUGH I WAS ZIGGY STARDUST, NEVER REALIZING DAVID JONES MIGHT BE BEHIND IT. I WAS ZONKED OUT OF MY MIND."
DAVID BOWIE

DAVID BOWIE CROONING.

might succumb to seductive, fascinating ideas; especially those that promised salvation, inner strength and the possibility of revenge on the hordes of enemies he now felt sure were plotting against him. Many of Bowie's music business friends – especially John Lennon and Elton John – became increasingly concerned for his state of mental and physical health. Yet despite the realities of the of the problems he faced there was always a nagging feeling that Bowie may once again have been acting out a role.

Throughout this time Bowie continued to work relentlessly. With a new-found enthusiasm for performing, on February 2, 1976 he embarked on his first world tour for two years. At the same time, he began planning a new life, shipping the contents of his Hollywood home to a new base in Switzerland. However, by September of that year he had moved to Berlin where he leased the apartment where he would lived for the next two-and-a-half years.

Bowie's stay in Germany saw him produce the albums *Low* and *Heroes* – part of a crucial and influential phase in an ever-changing career. Perhaps , then, *Station To Station* is best viewed as an interim album. But it still had the power to move Bowie ever onwards in his quest for fame and fortune, driven by the need to solve all those mysteries of life.

STATION TO STATION

This is an important piece of work in which first impressions can be singularly deceptive. The constant blending of influences, half-formed ideas, secret messages and occasional glimmers of light make Bowie's recorded performances a rich resource for speculation and debate. All aboard? Bowie is about to take us on a wild ride aboard an electronically-emulated steam train. At least these are the sound effects heard in the extended introduction. It takes a long while to build up a piece that signals the departure of the Bowie Express to whatever strange new destinations await the listener. The German electronic synthesizer band Kraftwerk, who had enjoyed a unexpected international hit single with an intriguing track called 'Autobahn' during 1975, probably influenced this locomotive device.

Stranger still, 'Station To Station' is one title track that was not a hit single. Although the album eventually yielded at least one hit in the form of the single 'Golden Years' – it would be many years before Bowie once again became a regular fixture in the international charts.

It was all part of his increasing alienation from the superficial and predictable rock world, a process that evidently began at this time and led to experimental work on his next three albums. As the train rushes through the stations, a ticking clock is summoned, courtesy of the plinking keyboards, guitar, drums and bass that gradually come into play. Some observers simply saw the locomotive sounds as a simulation of the coast-to-coast train journey Bowie endured when he refused to fly from New York to LA.

GERMAN TECHNO
BOYS KRAFTWERK.

Others felt it represented his intended flight or escape from America to Europe. There are no vocals for several minutes until Bowie emerges from the hubbub to pronounce "The return of the thin white duke, throwing darts in lovers' eyes".

He sings this beautifully – the initial desultory theme is abandoned and the tempo doubles. Bowie begins an exultant reprimand, chanting: "Too late – to be grateful... too late – to be hateful – the European cannon is here." At this time in his career, Bowie was beginning to study religion avidly and it may be that he is actually meaning the word "canon" as in a church decree regulating morals and religious practices. "Stations" could also have a religious meaning, as in "Stations of The Cross", of which there are 14 – each "station" representing some incident in the passage of Christ from the judgment hall to Calvary. They start with Christ's condemnation to death, progress to his nailing to the cross and conclude with the deposition in the sepulchre. At each station, prayers are offered.

While this isn't offered as a literal explanation for the song, 'Station To Station' is about transformation and travel. After all, Bowie was about to make his great journey from the New World back to the Old.

The whole piece shifts into a different gear half way through proceedings. It becomes a strange mixture of rock guitar and Georgio Moroder-style disco rhythm in which the good old US-style guitar is so much at odds with the Euro beat, it almost sounds like it is being played in a different key. Alienation strikes again. Bowie beats up on his vocal delivery too.

Although the vocals are some-what buried in the mix, something he was to complain about later, it is possible to detect those curious turns of phrase that hint at his state of mind and physical condition. At one point you hear him blurt out: "It's not the side effects of the cocaine, I'm thinking that it must be love," insisting that his deepest motivation comes from love rather than drugs.

Religion, drugs, love, fame, money: it's a heady cocktail for anyone to imbibe, let alone try to encompass in song. "I must explain that I don't necessarily know what I'm talking about in my writing," commented Bowie. "All I try to do is assemble points that interest me and puzzle through it and that becomes a song. Other people who listen to that song must take what they can from it and see if the information they've assembled fits in with anything I've assembled. I cannot say 'This is where it's at' because I don't know!"

Sometimes a harsh critic of his own work, Bowie was generally pleased with 'Station To Station': "I liked it. I wish I'd done it differently though. I compromised in the mixing. I wanted to do a dead mix. It should have been a dry mix. All the way through, no echo." He continued: "All the way through the making of the album I was telling myself I'd do a dry mix. And I gave in; I gave in and added that extra commercial touch. I wish I hadn't. 'Station To Station' was like a plea to come back to Europe for me. It was one of those self-chat things that one has with oneself from time to time."

While this was seen as the general thrust of the entire album, the title song also seems to allude in some way to Bowie's age-old problem of connecting with true love in order to alleviate his all-consuming loneliness. The paradox, however, is that the Thin White Duke always ends up by shattering his hopes of finding such love by his remoteness. Yet at the same time, there is always hope, there is light, there will always be many new mountains to conquer and human aspiration will soar, come what may.

THE GOLDEN YEARS

David Bowie's only hit from *Station To Station* was eventually issued as a single coupled with 'Can You Hear Me' in November, 1975, peaking at Number 10 in the US *Billboard* chart. It was his first hit in America since 'Fame' and would be his last until 'Under Pressure', a collaboration with Queen, scraped into the Top 30 in 1981.

This performance has more in common with the Philly soul groove of '*Young Americans*' – indeed, the song was offered to fellow RCA artiste Elvis Presley, who turned it down. Just a month after 'Space Oddity' had returned to the UK charts, where it went to the Number 1 spot, 'Golden Years' only managed to reach Number 8, which must have been both frustrating and confusing for Bowie.

A hand-clapping ditty that relies mainly on the soporific chant of the hook line, 'Golden Years' is a pleasant enough piece of work in contrast with the general thrust of the album. On one level a radio-friendly foot stomper, it also hints at the composer's fear of failure, even while he is simultaneously being feted as a megastar.

Bowie wrote the song as a tribute to his wife Angie, no doubt in a moment of nostalgia for the good old days. After he'd finished the demo he played the song over the phone to her including the line "I'll stick with you baby for a thousand years, nothing's gonna touch you in these golden years."

It's said that Angie believed in the song so much that she personally delivered the demo to Elvis Presley.

WORD ON A WING

In 'Word On A Wing', Bowie returns to a highly-mannered style of vocalizing that is impressive, yet occasionally irritating. His fellow musicians must have sometimes wondered what planet he was on when he went into this kind of warbling theatrical overdrive. Forgivable maybe in a neurotic younger man, but Bowie was approaching middle age and such histrionics did not really wash anymore. That said, the hymn-like qualities of this religious ballad are appealing, and Roy Bittan's piano work is excellent. The composer described the song as being about "the acceptance of the inevitable" but it is also about the search for a solution to man's problems through religion. "Just because I believe don't mean I don't think as well."

The choral backing adds to the curious atmosphere, as if Bowie had entered the church of the insane. One day he would get down on his knees and recite The Lord's Prayer at a rock concert, in memory of Freddie Mercury. He later told *New Musical Express*: "It was the first time I really thought seriously about Christ and God in any depth and 'Word On A Wing' was a protection." He revealed that while filming *The Man Who Fell To Earth* he often experienced strange terrors that led him to wear a silver crucifix around his neck for protection. "The song was something I needed to produce from within myself to safeguard myself against some of the situations that I felt were happening on the film set."

TVC15

In 'TVC15', Bowie reaches out from the depth of his Cherokee studio and anticipates the future of pop music, a musical form that is at once rootless, shiftless and meaningless. Here, in 1975, he creates a sound and philosophy that would work as well in 1999. Despite all the arguments and debates about the meaning of *Station To Station* as an advanced concept, this is not techno. It is not disco and it's not even rock 'n' roll. It is pop art by numbers. "Transition! Transmission!" yells Bowie. And that's it. Kraftwerk meets Mungo Jerry. Eurotrash meets Professor Longhair. So where does he go from here? The producer figured the song was about a TV set that eats his girlfriend, echoing a scene in *The Man Who Fell To Earth* where Bowie is absorbed by rows of TV screens. It has been postulated that the song was originally intended for Bowie's unrealized movie soundtrack.

It's certainly not the sort of material to start a youth crusade. It does signal the arrival of pop music as a background roar of static, like the noise of the Big Bang that permeates outer space. And it's all because Bowie used the "cut up" techniques again, borrowed from his favourite sci-fi author William Burroughs, who developed the theory that true communication through language was impossible because it consists merely of coded expressions that only get the responses they demand and deserve. The idea is that by reducing the power of words, true feelings and consciousness can be liberated. Although 'TVC15' was released as a single coupled with 'We Are The Dead' in April, 1976, as part of the promotion for the European tour, it failed to get any higher in the UK chart than Number 33.

STAY

Kick-ass drums are the highlight of this intriguing "Son of Fame". It's a piece of pure funk on which the singer, by now somewhat tired and emotional, takes a welcome back seat. That's not to say he doesn't make a reasonable contribution, singing: "You can never really tell when somebody wants something or wants to stay!" Wafting a breath of fresh air, Bowie launches into a flow of basic, simple and direct lyrics that address the problems of nervous suitors everywhere. Well, are you going to stay the night or not? But the real excitement begins when Bowie slopes off for a quick cigarette behind the control booth and the band get stuck into a jam session powered by Alomar's fidgety guitar licks. A great closer at concerts, this track is still regarded as one of Bowie's most appealing, least difficult numbers from the Seventies. Yet when it was released in the US as a single, coupled with 'Word On A Wing', in August, 1976, it failed to make any impression on the chart.

WILD IS THE WIND

There is a vocal technique that requires sticking your tongue out and allowing the air to blast forth from the back of the throat. It produces the kind of deep-toned, almost lugubrious, style that is employed here by the singer, who seems to be plunging ever-deeper into a slough of despond. With overtones of John Leyton's 'Johnny Remember Me', this is a modest little ballad that makes a rather odd ending to a distinctly strange album. It seems like Bowie is saying farewell to America, farewell to rock and farewell to the musicians who had served him so well over the previous few years. Indeed this was the last album he would record in America for another four years.

Written by Dimitri Tiomkin for the 1957 film *Wild Is The Wind*, starring Anthony Quinn and Anna Magnani, the theme song was first recorded by balladeer Johnny Mathis. The wind in question is the inspirational power of love that blows through the heart. It's rendered rather tedious and silly in Bowie's version – he pauses to utter the emotion-charged phrase "Don't you know you are life itself", a delivery that would have been greeted with a cry of "Next!" at any repertory theatre audition.

Station To Station gradually fades into darkness as the studio lights go out, leaving only the glowing cigarette-end of the singer, as he muses on his next move and the prospect of pastures new.

PUTTING THE WIND UP BOWIE. PARAMOUNT MOVIE POSTER (1956).

The CD reissue of *Station To Station* included live versions of 'Word On A Wing' and 'Stay', recorded at the Nassau Coliseum, Long Island in March, 1976, giving fresh insight into the increasingly strange musical catalogue filed under "Bowie".

123

LOW

Released	January 1977
Produced by	David Bowie & Tony Visconti
Recorded at	Recorded at the Chateau d'Herouville France and Hansa By The Wall, Berlin, Germany
Musicians	David Bowie (vocals, guitar, pump bass, saxophones, xylophones, vibraphones, harmonica, ARP synthesizer, piano, Chamberlin) Carlos Alomar, Ricky Gardiner (guitar) George Murray (bass) Dennis Davis (percussion) Roy Young (piano, Farfisa organ) Peter Himmelman (piano, ARP synthesizer) Eduard Meyer (cello) Mary Visconti, Iggy Pop (backing vocals)

SPEED OF LIFE

BREAKING GLASS

WHAT IN THE WORLD

SOUND AND VISION

ALWAYS CRASHING IN THE SAME CAR

BE MY WIFE

A NEW CAREER IN A NEW TOWN

WARSZAWA

ART DECADE

WEEPING WALL

SUBTERRANEANS

DAVID BOWIE: THE EPITOME OF COOL.

"Rock Is Dead!" Roared David Bowie. "Long Live Rock!" Bellowed Pete Townshend. These dramatic pronouncements to a breathless world came during a battle of ideology at the height of the booming Seventies. The pressure was on to maintain the status quo. Rock music had enjoyed huge popularity for a decade. The Who and Led Zeppelin were at the peak of their powers, and there was a boom in sales. So why rock the boat? Bowie was bored. He wanted out. Rock 'n' roll had been good for him, but he was desperate to break free and find a new direction. He'd done the blockbuster albums. There was no point in repeating himself. *Station to Station* had given him breathing space. Now it was time to relaunch himself – this time into outer space. So was rock dead? So far as many thinking musicians were concerned it was already consigned to the Stone Age. The race was on to create a new kind of music and, predictably, David Bowie was among the first out of the gate.

In 1977 Bowie was determined to draw a line under his past and reinvent himself. He had left America to live in Europe. He had split with his manager and was growing further apart from his wife. He had done so much and lived so hard that the only sensible thing to do now was rebuild his life, his business, his image and his music. To an intelligent and sensitive man like Bowie it was obvious that the only way to find satisfaction and a degree of happiness was to move on. He had quickly grown tired of the superficial life of a pop star while living in Los Angeles.

There were also sound business reasons for making changes. He had been the plaything of Svengali-type managers for too long. He began managing himself and proudly said: "I've got complete control and it's never been better. I know exactly what I'm doing and it's fun. It's a bit tiring because I'm working 24 hours a day but it's worth it because I'm making the money and keeping it this time." In the past he alleged that he was making money mainly to support "60-piece road crews"; from here on, Bowie pared down his touring staff to the bare minimum.

'Fame' and *Young Americans* had brought him the recognition and rewards he had long sought, but he couldn't go on playing "plastic soul" any more than he could keep up his carefully contrived dramatic roles – Thin White Duke included.

Since the beginning of the decade, Bowie had managed to work with some marvellously responsive musicians, among them Mick Ronson and Carlos Alomar. Now two new men came into his life: Brian Eno and Robert Fripp were the British artists able to provide the impetus and support for the next phase in his extraordinary career.

**CARLOS ALOMAR
GOES GUITAR CRAZY.**

The superheated rock music, predicated on the blues and pop revolution of the Sixties, seemed all-powerful and important during the Seventies. However, there were other strands of musical and technical development that were creeping up on a music business often slow to recognize the imminent changes. While rock seemed secure in its basic guitar, bass and drums format with a long-haired singer screaming up front, there were other ways of making pop music that did not need to rely on traditional methods. Most rock musicians despised disco and looked askance at drum machines and synthesizers. Yet the tight rhythms demanded by disco and dance music in a strange way created their own liberating force. You only have to listen to the drumming on Bowie's albums like *Young Americans* and *Station To Station* and compare them to his previous records to realize the improvements. Those musicians aware of the shift in emphasis were getting slicker, more responsive, less clumsy and less inept. The race was on between the human players and the machines to see who could be the most efficient in the studio. Ultimately the machines won, and popular music would never be the same again. It was a development that began with albums like *Low*. Yet, strangely enough, the power of rock was also revived, thanks to new production methods employed on a substantial chunk of the new Bowie album. Rock was not quite dead – it was just being given the kiss of life.

Low was a poor seller compared to Bowie's previous albums, although it did sell enough to go "Gold". Understandably, when RCA executives first heard the tapes they were in shock. One executive went so far as to tell Bowie to get back to Los Angeles and make a hit album again – one they could sell. Calls went out to his old manager Tony Defries to see if he could get Bowie to put some vocals on the many tracks that appeared to be solely instrumental. Their disenchantment was understandable. Just as Bowie had reorganized his life, so he had restructured his writing, with the invaluable assistance of Eno, the man who was devising a new sound and approach that became known as "ambient music". Gone were the up-beat traditional pop songs and even the Dylanesque narratives of yore. Even the disco funk of 'Fame', revolutionary in its way, was superseded by a more rambling, desultory kind of performance.

ROBERT FRIPP:
GUITAR PIONEER.

Even today, if you play *Low* to young musicians unfamiliar with the album, the response tends to be: "This is not going anywhere" or "it sounds like a band that hasn't played together before." – it's the second decade of the 21st century, and *Low* still has the capacity to confuse and disturb. A lot of the time Bowie sounds like he's not even there.

When he does sing it is in a series of muttered asides, in a made-up language, or a limited number of intelligible verses. This is the sound, literally, of a man in a room, locked away, undergoing therapy and not wanting to interact with anyone except the people already in the room. The outside world, noisy and demanding, can wait.

Bowie put forward one reason for the new approach: "In LA I fell into the trap of referring back to rock all the time. I had blinkered myself to all other musical possibilities. When I left, I tried to find out more about The World. I discovered how little I knew, how little I had to say. The lyrics on *Low* reflect that I was literally stuck for words. I was making a new musical language for my new life."

The bravery of Bowie in taking this step is, in retrospect, quite breathtaking. Together with Eno and Tony Visconti, Bowie forged a new way of looking at making records. Instead of sticking to the tried and obvious, they had the courage to think afresh. And it is astonishing how many facets of the *Low* concept were subsequently absorbed into the mainstream. These included the dominance of relentless, crashing drums, the off-key guitar, simplistic synthesizer and keyboard riffs; the lifeless, emotion-drained vocals, the pared-down lyrics and the on-going blurring of vocal parts into a deep instrumental hypnosis. Bowie's significant partner in this new venture was Brian Peter George St Baptiste de la Salle Eno (born May 15, 1948, in Woodbridge, Suffolk, England) – known to the world simply as "Eno".

Eno studied art and could not play an instrument. But he was influenced by the avant garde music of composers Cornelius Cardew and John Cage, and he played around making diverse sounds with multitrack tape recorders. He even published a ground-breaking book in 1968 called *Music for Non-Musicians*. Eno spent some time working with experimental groups and performing avant garde music before joining Roxy Music, in 1971, as their technical adviser. The striking figure, with his long blond hair, became popular with fans and almost upstaged the lead singer Bryan Ferry – which may have contributed to Eno's departure from the group in June, 1973. In the aftermath he launched his solo career, and began working with King Crimson's guitarist, Robert Fripp. In November that year they went on tour together and produced an album called *No Pussyfooting*.

In the course of the next two years Eno released *Here Come the Warm Jets* (1974), with lyrics and vocals, set up his own recording label, and worked with John Cale, Kevin Ayers, Nico and Mike Oldfield. In 1975 he released *Another Green World* – an album that had an effect on David Bowie. Eno also performed with Phil Manzanera's group 801, and worked with the painter, Peter Schmidt, on a concept called "Oblique Strategies" (designed to promote lateral thinking, it involved a series of cards). It was around that time that he began to collaborate with Bowie on the series of albums – *Low*, *Heroes* and *Lodger* – which Bowie refers to as "the Berlin triptych".

Although Bowie's wife Angela had set up a home for him in Switzerland, which became his official base after he left America, he preferred to live in an apartment in Berlin that he occasionally shared with his old friend Iggy Pop. At first he did nothing and just gave himself time and space to think. He described his Hollywood sojourn as "One of the worst periods of my life. I got into a lot of emotional and spiritual trouble there, and so I decided to split and discover new ways of relating to the music business. I wasn't exactly sure what I was in it for any more. The first thing I did when I got back to Europe was to stop thinking about music and performing for a bit and think about something else." He began to spend more time painting, which helped to calm him down and even got him back into music, albeit in a different form.

Berlin seemed an alien, remote place as far as most young Western rock fans were concerned. It was still behind the Iron Curtain and surrounded by a hostile East Germany. An outpost of capitalism, it was a divided city, with the infamous Berlin Wall providing a constant reminder of Soviet dominance.

129

Bowie was the first international rock star to take up residence there. He lived in a quiet area, renting a comfortable apartment from which he ventured forth by bicycle, hoping to blend in with the locals, and partially disguised with a newly-grown moustache and cap. Although his presence was reported in the local press, he did achieve a degree of anonymity and peace. Drawn to the city by its atmosphere, and its traditions of art, literature and cabaret, Bowie found there were as many museums and galleries to visit as nightclubs. This was the Berlin of Christopher Isherwood and Marlene Dietrich, that had been celebrated on a Lou Reed album called simply *Berlin*. It was an ideal place to be a creative artist. Bowie lived in Berlin, off and on, for the next three years and it was where he took his young son Joe to live after the final acrimonious divorce from Angie.

During a break in his World Tour, in April, 1976, Bowie took a trip to Moscow and was held on a train at the Polish/Russian border by customs officers searching his luggage. After completing his British shows in London in May he went to the Chateau d'Herouville, near Paris, France where he had previously worked on *Pin Ups*, and produced Iggy Pop's new album, *The Idiot*, on which he co-wrote most of the songs and played sax and guitar. Bowie later toured anonymously with Iggy as his on-stage keyboard player and, for a while, he seemed to prefer to promote Iggy's career.

In September, Bowie began work at the Chateau again, this time on his own album, provisionally titled *New Music, Night And Day*. Tony Visconti was invited to be the producer and the musicians taking part included remnants of the *Station To Station* band with Carlos Alomar (guitar), Ricky Gardener (guitars), Dennis Davis (percussion) and George Murray (bass), together with Roy Young (piano). Bowie played a variety of instruments while Eno added piano, Mini-Moog and various other synthesizers. Although he's not credited on the record, some of the guitar parts sound like the work of Robert Fripp. Carlos Alomar was featured on eight of the tracks, continuing the good work he had done with Bowie since 1975 both in the studio and on tour, and became Bowie's trusted musical arranger,.

Conditions at the Chateau were not too good because most of the staff were away on holiday and there was little in the way of food available. Bowie also had to go into Paris for several business meetings with his ex-manager, Michael Lippman – meetings that proved stressful.

These were some of the pressures that led Bowie to rename the album *Low* in reflection of the way he felt after several tough confrontations. Following an outbreak of dysentery at the studio, caused by a faulty water supply, Bowie relocated to Berlin and work continued at the Hansa By The Wall studios.

"THE LYRICS ON LOW REFLECT THAT I WAS LITERALLY STUCK FOR WORDS. I WAS MAKING A NEW MUSICAL LANGUAGE FOR MY NEW LIFE." DAVID BOWIE

The music was divided into two halves, with the rockier music concentrated on Side One and the more experimental work featured on Side Two. One of the key elements of the sound on the "rock" side was the drumming of Dennis Davis, almost as powerful as that achieved by John Bonham on certain Led Zeppelin tracks produced by Jimmy Page. However, Tony Visconti produced his own extra special drum sound on *Low*.

Visconti said later that he had stumbled on the huge snare-drum sound by accident. He explained that when the Eventide company bought out a new studio device called a Harmonizer he ordered one for use at home. "I was told I had the second one in the country. I played with it solidly for about a week, putting every sound source I could think of through it so I could hear what it could do. I noticed that if you put a snare through it and dropped the pitch, and then fed it back into the desk, it made this great "ground" sound. When Bowie asked me to go to France to do *Low* with him I took the Harmonizer with me. Bowie's drummer Dennis Davis went crazy when he first heard the sound in the cans and he completely rearranged his fills."

Tony kept his technique a secret for a year while his rival producers felt sure he had achieved the drum sound by using compressors and echo chambers and had somehow recorded it all backwards. In fact, he had done it all with an off-the-shelf piece of gear. The enhanced drum sound proved very influential. Peter Gabriel and Phil Collins used an equally powerful effect on 'Intruder' a track on the 1980 album, *Peter Gabriel*. Throughout the Eighties and even more so today, the heavy drum sound became crucial to both rock, pop and dance records. Bowie was rather dismissive of this sound but only when it became apparent that everyone else was bent on copying the approach that he called "that depressive Gorilla effect". He added: "It was something I wished we'd never created, having had to live through years of it with other English bands."

Equally important, of course, was the collaboration with Eno, who was surprised to discover that both Bowie and Iggy Pop were familiar with *No Pussyfooting*. They could hum all the themes, note-for-note. Bowie had first met Brian Eno when Roxy Music had played support during the Ziggy era and Bowie stayed in touch, keeping a close watch on Eno's development. Eno enjoyed working with Bowie and had been very impressed by Bowie's most recent *Station To Station* album. He said later, to rock writer Miles: "We worked very well together. David works very fast. He's very impulsive and works like crazy for about two hours and then takes the rest of the day off." Eno, by contrast, worked more slowly, using his synthesizer to build up the tracks one line at a time. While Bowie was in Paris attending to legal matters,

Eno worked on alone, creating a couple of pieces for Bowie to hear on his return, one of which was the hotly-debated 'Warszawa'.

Bowie liked them, added vocals and put them on the album. Eno was at the Chateau for just a week in September, where nine of the eleven tracks were recorded, and then Visconti and Bowie went to Berlin to complete mixing and recording the remaining two tracks.

Said Bowie: "Of all the people that I've heard who write textures, Brian Eno's textures always appealed to me the most. Brian isn't interested in context. He's a man with peculiar notions, some of which I can come to terms with very easily and are most accessible and some of it is way above my head in terms of his analytical studies of cybernetics and his application of those things to music."

Although much of the material was written and recorded in France, Bowie has said that living in Berlin was the catalyst for the mood of the album. West Berlin was a lively, thriving, modern, neon-lit metropolis, stocked with luxuries and full of affluence. On the other side of the wall, in East Berlin, the architecture was Stalinist, there were still vast bombsites and at night they turned off the traffic lights to save electricity.

Bowie, in common with most Western visitors, found visits behind the Iron Curtain into the East sobering and alarming experiences. Even living in Berlin's more comfortable and lively Western sector produced a strange sense of isolation and danger. Passengers landing at the Templehof airport could sometimes hear machine gun fire nearby. Said Bowie: "That initial period of living in Berlin produced *Low*. It was like 'Isn't it great being on your own? Let's just pull down the blinds and fuck 'em all.' The first side of *Low* was all about me, but Side Two was more an observation in musical terms – my reaction to seeing the Eastern bloc, how West Berlin survived in the middle of it which was something that I couldn't express in words."

Despite the gloom that permeated some of the tracks it wasn't all despondency in the studios. Bowie confirmed that Robert Fripp had been present during the making of *Low* when he described the atmosphere and fun that they had making the record. "We spent most of our time joking, laughing and falling on the floor. I think out of all the time we spent recording, 40 minutes out of every hour was spent just crying with laughter. Fripp is incredibly funny, with an unbelievable sense of humour."

The album was completed in time for a proposed Christmas release, but when RCA heard it they weren't best pleased and it wasn't released until January 1977. Attempts were even made behind the scenes to prevent it coming out at all – those hoping for a new version of *Young Americans* volunteered to buy Bowie a house in Philadelphia so he could get back into that "Philly groove".

The album came in a bland orange cover distinguished only by a discrete profile picture of Bowie taken from *The Man Who Fell To Earth*. It was perhaps Bowie's way of hinting that this could have been the soundtrack album of the movie, if certain people had just done their homework. The colour picture presents Bowie as particularly vulnerable, with strands of hair falling over his ears, lips drawn and red, the collar of a windcheater turned up around his neck, as if to protect him from the chill blasts of winter. Now was the winter of his discontent".

The reviews for the album were mixed, and as Bowie didn't do any interviews to promote the record, it tended to get lost and forgotten amid the fuss over the so-called New Wave of British punk rock. With the Sex Pistols grabbing all the headlines and attention, it wasn't the best of times for Bowie to put out an album of "difficult", cerebral art-rock. He even went so far as to say he didn't care if it sold or not – spoken like a true creative artist. Even so, it still hurt when so many either grumbled about the album or just ignored and forgot about its existence.

Bowie expressed his feelings about the general reaction later in the year. "I was disappointed at the reception *Low* got from the press. I gave them more credit for that. A lot of people dismissed it as an Eno album. Obviously he was very important to *Low* but I put a lot of blood and guts into that album, a fact that tends to be ignored."

What could definitely not be ignored was the fact that, despite the lack of promotion and publicity, one of the tracks was a palpable chart hit. 'Sound And Vision' miraculously got to Number 3 shortly after entering the UK chart in February, 1977, but did less well in the US. In a year that saw The Muppets and the Sex Pistols dominating the album charts, such was Bowie's magical hold on his audience that, despite bad reviews, *Low* got to Number 2 in the UK album charts and reached Number 11 in the US. Not such a disaster, not such a failure. More, as critics later came to agree, "one of Bowie's most important albums".

SPEED OF LIFE

So what's wrong with a crashing work-out with an addictive rock riff that sounds like the Rolling Stones meets Velvet Underground? Bowie plays the melody on synthetic strings and an "ARP Tape Horn". Vocals – who needs them? Not when the guys are busy rocking out and Carlos Alomar's guitar is smoking. Bowie is clearly engrossed and enjoying himself making music. Listen to that Tape Horn go! Also worth noting is the descending thermionic-valve-sound synth line, which was later revived for use on 'Scary Monsters'. This opening cut helps set the mood for the rest of Side One, a series of sketches, all imbued with the same aggressive drumming, adopting a slightly ramshackle approach and with a curious sense of detachment emanating from the composer. Although the mood is supposed to be "*low*", you can hear the humour that Bowie describes; the sort of comradeship among the musicians that makes this a piece that everyone just wants to go on playing, until the tape runs out, whirling at the speed of life.

BREAKING GLASS

Remember Dread Zeppelin? They came knocking on our doors 20 years later with the same manic mixtures of influences, grooves and hot drums that Bowie introduced on *Low*.

Here is another rock-solid stomp, with Dennis Davis hammering his drums with a kind of brute strength not normally recommended in *The Art Of Drumming – Book 1*. Bowie pokes his head around the studio door, and pops up at the microphone. "Baby I've been breaking glass in your room again. Listen don't look at the carpet I drew something awful on it... Such a wonderful person, but you got problems – oh, oh, oh, oh..." he whoops. This sudden vocal interjection in a piece that fades out almost before it has begun is oddly tantalizing. You want to hear the whole story. The "wonderful person", we may infer, is Angie, but goodness knows what Bowie was drawing on her carpet.

Oddly enough, despite all the fuss about Eno's involvement with *Low*, he hardly makes an appearance on these introductory items, content to add some Mini Moog. Let's face it, Bowie's old mate Rick Wakeman could easily have done that – his involvement might also have brought about a version of *Low* On Ice at the Empire Pool, London, although this might have had those more acerbic critics doing something even worse on the carpet. This piece, which lasts a mere 102 seconds, was credited not to Eno but to Bowie, Davis and Alomar. A few years later, a pop star was born when Hazel O'Connor starred in a highly-acclaimed punk rock movie called *Breaking Glass* (1980). Bowie's glass-breaking, however, was more to do with his battles to escape relationships that weren't working.

WHAT IN THE WORLD

Wallop! Bash! Dennis Davis sets the pace as Bowie picks up the vocals and suddenly seems bent on producing a period-piece pop song with distinct Sixties overtones. When he repeats the phrase that he is in the mood "For your love", you picture him craning his neck, as a young lad at the Marquee Club, watching Keith Relf and The Yardbirds, who had a big hit in 1965 called 'For Your Love'.

The full complement of Chateau d'Herouville regulars is on hand, including Iggy Pop adding vocals. The pair of reprobates sing about "a little girl with grey eyes" who never leaves her room but is urged to wait until the crowd goes when Bowie, who is a little bit afraid of her, can get to know her better and engage in meaningful conversation, probably about sex. The tune was performed on Bowie's subsequent tour in 1978, on *Serious Moonlight* in 1983 and again during the 1995 *Outside* outing.

SOUND AND VISION

A reggae-style whack on a choke cymbal offsets the lilting beat that characterizes the hit theme from this unnervingly unpredictable sequence of songs. "Ah, um" is Bowie's concession to words, after several bars of Alomar guitar riffing, interspersed by that old familiar detuned Bowie sax.

"Don't you wonder sometimes about sound and vision," sings Bowie briefly, probably thinking about the sign that flashes on and off in BBC TV studios, or did in the days of *Muffin The Mule, Whirligig* and *What's My Line*. Interestingly enough, in 1977 this was picked up by the BBC and used as background music during announcements for a while, probably at the behest of Alan "Cracked Actor" Yentob.

What this song says is simple. You don't need to write a triple-concept album about mutant rats or peoploids to maintain a life in pop. You can mutter a few words, sing along to a silly tune that could be a nursery rhyme, and still get a hefty advance. "Blue, blue, electric blue, that's the colour of my room, where I will live," sings Bowie, peeping out from behind the net curtains and making himself a nice cup of tea. Eno joins in the vocals here, together with Mary Visconti – better known to pop-pickers as Mary Hopkin.

There are still no signs of the much vaunted "oblique strategies" at work, but this was, nonetheless, the big hit that everyone was looking for.

ALWAYS CRASHING IN THE SAME CAR

A touch of Jo-Meek-style wobbly space noise (could this be one of Eno's oblique strategies?) helps launch another strangely affecting Bowie theme. Always looking backwards, always looking forwards – it's the story of David Bowie's life.

It's strange that in the middle of all the synthesizers and spooky sounds on offer here, the whole piece, rather like its predecessor 'Sound And Vision', is nonetheless pure, classic pop – structurally speaking, at least.

The guitar solo sounds oddly like Peter Banks (of Yes fame) at work, complete with jokey string-bending, which leads one to suspect that this might be a Robert Fripp solo tacked on – Fripp being one of Banks's big influences. However, Ricky Gardener is credited as the lead player with Carlos Alomar on rhythm.

Bowie described this song as being part of his tendency towards "self-pitying crap" but he undersells himself. Bowie mutters the desultory, introspective phrases summing up the inevitability of crisis, which occur even when he tries so hard to be a decent, regular guy.

BE MY WIFE

Criticized for being "mawkish", this is actually rather a sad and moving little song. Bowie cries out: "Sometimes you get so lonely... I've lived all over the world... please be mine... be my wife". It's all the more affecting when you know that he was still actually married to Angie at the time. Of course, the singer could be anyone delivering a universal message of loneliness on behalf of the lost and dispirited.

Bowie sings in a pleasing manner that is beguiling in its innocence, almost a throwback to the young Mod wandering the streets of London in 1967 in search of love. "It was genuinely anguished," Bowie said later, "but I think it could have been about anybody."

'Be My Wife' was released as a single in June, 1977, coupled with 'Speed Of Life', but it only reached the bottom end of the charts. Surprisingly, given his previous decision not to promote the album by giving interviews, Bowie turned up on BBC TV's *Top Of The Pops* to sing the number, which was his first solo appearance (apart from the Iggy tour) for some long time.

A NEW CAREER IN A NEW TOWN

This track provides an exceptionally strong ending to Side One – an ending that makes you wonder why everyone at RCA was panicking quite so much about the content of the album.

So what's wrong with this arrangement? Okay, it sounds a bit like 'Groovin' With Mr Bloe', a 1970 Number 2 UK hit by the redoubtable Mr Bloe, but that's mainly because of the heavy use of harmonica, which is oddly out of context among the ticking bass rhythms and heavy-handed pub piano. The main problem, of course, is the complete absence of any vocalizing by the man who once sang 'Space Oddity', 'Queen Bitch', and 'Is There Life On Mars?'. That un-Earthly being from long ago and far away has left the stage.

WARSZAWA

Although some critics said *Low* was more an Eno than a Bowie album, this was the only composition that was actually given a co-credit to Bowie-Eno. This is where Eno finally comes into the big picture, his strangely-named "Oblique Strategies" at the ready. These were special, randomly selected "oracle" cards, containing instructions and aphorisms designed to help the creative process. Eno had used them with Roxy Music, and they include messages such as "go slowly all the way round the outside" and "disconnect from desire".

Bowie had visited the capital of Poland on a trip in April, 1976. "'Warszawa' is about Warsaw and the very bleak atmosphere I got from that city. It was quite a positive idea to try and take a musical picture of the countryside of Poland. But I didn't tell Brian that. The procedure of that was quite simple. I said 'Look Brian I want to compose a really slow piece of music but I want a very emotive, almost religious feel to it. That's all I want to tell you at this point.'" Bowie asked for suggestions and Eno decided to lay down a track of finger clicks. He laid down 430 clicks on a clean tape. They then put them all out as dots on a piece of paper and numbered them all off. Bowie picked sections of dots and Eno picked sections too. Eno went back into the studio and played chords and changed the chords as he hit the particular number. "I did a similar thing on my areas. We then took the clicks out, heard the piece of music as was, and then wrote over the top of that, according to the length of bars we'd given ourselves," Bowie explained.

The piece reflected Bowie's musings on the country he explored, having read about Poland's chequered history. He may have mused on the tragedy of life and death in the Jewish Ghetto that was set up in Warsaw following the German invasion and the city's destruction in the aerial blitzkrieg that started World War II. Certainly there is much room for personal interpretation. Bowie leaves space for the imagination to wander, by singing in a language of his own devising, perhaps Polish, perhaps even Ishkatar, the tongue employed by the hermits of Hertzogovenia.

ART DECADE

Art Decade' is another intriguing voyage into the world of the unfettered tone poem. The cello is played by studio engineer Eduard Meyer, on a piece that takes in decadence, art deco and those decades of creativity when Berlin was the heartland of all such things. A time when the young folk painted, danced, drank and laughed their way to impending oblivion while the drums of war beat ever louder. A time when the men folk began to pack up their old kit bags, and the women wept for times past. All this and much more.

WEEPING WALL

This is Bowie's baby, a piece that bubbles, gurgles and bounces as it blends together pianos, synthetic strings, vibraphones, xylophones, and an ARP synthesizer. Bowie even tops up this entirely solo effort with some crying guitar and chilling vocals. This could be music for *The Man Who Fell To Earth* or even for the final moments of *2001: A Space Odyssey*. The pulsating tone that permeates the main theme is fascinating. Something similar was used many years later by drummer Vinnie Colaiuta on one of his showcase numbers. The avant garde composer Philip Glass was most impressed and later adapted some of Bowie's work from *Low*.

Although there is a Wailing Wall in Israel, this song is about the Berlin Wall, which claimed the lives of so many who tried to cross it and were shot by border guards, until it was finally torn down in 1989 in the lead-up to German reunification. Soon, the concrete structure which had inspired so much of this album, and put it into context, would become just a memory.

SUBTERRANEANS

This track was intended to be used in *The Man Who Fell To Earth* and it certainly has all the elements of isolation, loss of identity and mournful contemplation of the unhappy state of mind that such conditions bring in their wake. Lugubrious Bowie saxophone (still with that mouthpiece not firmly screwed into the cork as required) wails in the background, summoning images of pre-war Berlin, before The Wall divided the city. Eno is missing from this session, on which Carlos Alomar and George Murray joined Bowie. Rising and falling like the tide, the mood is unrelentingly gloomy but nonetheless valid and rewarding. As a tool for meditation and to lower your pulse rate, just lie in a prone position and fix your gaze upon a distant object while allowing 'Subterraneans' to wash over you. Unsurprisingly, this was not issued as a single. When the album was reissued on CD, in 1991, it contained the bonus tracks 'Some Are', 'All Saints', and a remix of 'Sound And Vision'.

"HEROES"

Released	October 1977
Produced by	David Bowie and Tony Visconti
Recorded at	Hansa By The Wall, Berlin, Germany
Musicians	David Bowie (vocals, keyboards, guitar, saxophone, koto)
	Carlos Alomar (rhythm guitar)
	Dennis Davis (percussion)
	George Murray (bass)
	Eno (synthesizers, keyboards, guitar treatments)
	Robert Fripp (lead guitar)
	Tony Visconti, Antonia Maass (backing vocals)

BEAUTY AND THE BEAST

JOE THE LION

"HEROES"

SONS OF THE SILENT AGE

BLACKOUT

V-2 SCHNEIDER

SENSE OF DOUBT

MOSS GARDEN

NEUKOLN

THE SECRET LIFE OF ARABIA

TRUE HEROES: BOWIE AND BOLAN ON MARC'S FINAL TV SHOW, SEPTEMBER 9, 1977.

"We can be heroes just for one day." There can be no more poignant anthem than David Bowie's stirring observation on the power of the human spirit.

Less bombastic than Freddie Mercury's "we are the champions", it has that same purposeful spirit of unity, the shared need to overcome adversity. Even though it was undoubtedly the best-known Bowie song of the era, it was not quite the major hit that had been anticipated. Indeed Bowie didn't conquer the US charts again until 1981 with 'Under Pressure', when he shared honours with Mercury's Queen. For a moment it looked as if phase two of the 'Berlin Triptych' would achieve the kind of anonymity that *Low* had presented as a virtue.

The delayed release of *Low*, early in the year, meant that Bowie had two albums out in 1977. The year began with the mixed reaction of critics to the album that RCA had tried to stall, and the comforting news that at least one track, 'Sound And Vision', had proved a hit. Bowie devoted his time to working with Iggy Pop, whose album *The Idiot* was released in March. Iggy Pop played six dates in the UK, with Bowie backing him on keyboards, followed by 16 dates in North America. In June, another *Low* track, 'Be My Wife', was released. In September, '"Heroes"', the single, was issued as a taster from the forthcoming album – the title was specifically set in inverted commas for reasons which will become clear.

Bowie saw *"Heroes"* as very much an extension of *Low* and, at the time, hinted that the next album would be in the same vein. "That's more out of spite than anything else, "he was heard to say, in biting reference to those who had tried to forestall his artistic endeavours and had poured scorn on his new musical direction. He assembled much the same team for *"Heroes"* as he'd used on *Low* and he featured himself on vocals, keyboards, guitar, saxophone and koto.

He was backed by the old firm of Carlos Alomar (rhythm guitar), Dennis Davis (percussion), George Murray (electric bass), Eno (synthesizers, keyboards and guitar treatments) and Robert Fripp on lead guitar. Recording took place at Hansa By The Wall studio in Berlin and mixing at Mountain Studios, Montreux, Switzerland. The Hansa studios were, quite literally, only a few yards from the Berlin Wall and it was possible to see the border guards glaring suspiciously from their watchtowers into the control room. It certainly added to the atmosphere of hostility and hastened the work schedule. Nobody really wanted to hang around for too long in such an environment.

The cover picture was one of Bowie's best in some years. A striking black and white shot, by photographer Sukita, depicted Bowie in a black leather jacket, one hand clutching his breast and the other held aloft. It was an artistic pose, similar in composition to a picture of Iggy Pop on *The Idiot*, who is seen holding his hands out in a different direction, more in the classic "got any spare change" position.

Bowie later commented that he thought his new album sounded fresh and imaginative. It wasn't a carefully contrived or preconceived piece of work. Indeed many of the lyrics were written in a trice. "I suppose it's not the happiest of albums but it wasn't all subjective. It was taken from observations. The lyrics on each track took five or six minutes to write and we were in the studio for a matter of a couple of weeks. If I'd been working on my own it wouldn't have been that long." Bowie consciously tried to avoid retakes, admitting that he got bored too quickly for such endless attention to details. This was a wise move – many Seventies rock groups foundered and broke up in the studios because of endless prevarication and a pointless search for perfection.

Large chunks of the music contained on *"Heroes"* were, if anything, even deeper, more esoteric and difficult to accept than the performances found on *Low*. It lacked the energy that side one of the previous album had espoused, and at least three pieces of the latest Bowie epic seemed deliberately designed to further alienate his long-suffering following. There was nothing wrong with these avant garde experiments – as an artist Bowie had every right to take this uncompromising path. But it was hard work for the average listener. People who loved Bowie, who had followed his career from the start and were prepared to put up with anything that had his name attached, were put off by the intensity of such works as 'Moss Garden' and what seemed like Bowie's darkest hour, 'Neukoln'. Looking on the brighter side of life, the album contained some up-beat material like 'Beauty And The Beast', and even the Kraftwerk-influenced 'V-2 Schneider' has its own mechanical charm. As was undoubtedly his intention, Bowie could not have got further away from the black soul of the American music tradition, whose music was largely steeped in humour, romance and humanity. Maybe he felt he had been overacting out the part of ersatz soul boy when he made records like *Young Americans*. With the success of artists like Rod Stewart and Elton John there was indeed a surfeit of Anglo Saxon, blue-eyed soul artists. Yet in going to the other extreme, there was a real danger of losing a grip on the mass market – a market that Bowie had massive difficulty winning over in the first place. Given that people had grown to accept surprise and change from Bowie as par for the course, it was perhaps a bigger surprise that he chose to stick with the Berlin influence for so long.

The sound of a neurotic koto and a tortured saxophone wasn't that appealing. Those who had mocked the image of A&R men trying to come to terms with *Low* began to feel a twinge of sympathy when Bowie plunged further into gloom on *"Heroes"*. You could have too much of a good thing. Maybe if he had chosen to live in Australia or Ireland, Bowie might have found a more positive and cheerful attitude to life. Instead of producing harrowing works like 'Sense Of Doubt' he might have joined an Aussie heavy-metal band, or recorded albums of pipe music with The Chieftains.

But Bowie had suffered a surfeit of jollity in Los Angeles and it's quite possible that even a trip to the more friendly and sociable regions of the globe might have tipped him over the edge. He needed time in a more neutral environment, where people go about their business and don't bother you or try to involve you in their lives. The Berlin suburbs proved ideal in this respect, as he explained: "It was a way of enabling me to associate again with a society I had initially shunned and was starting to feel I had permanently cut off. So it was a way of re-establishing myself as a citizen of some place." Bowie admits that at this time he had an enormous problem just communicating with people. (I attempted to speak to Bowie during his Berlin period. He looked up blankly and replied "That's very Polaroid man".)

"It was awfully hard to open up or let others open up to me. I found the Wall there, so it was quite ironic that I chose a city with this dividing wall to live in. But it did force me into confrontations with other people and normalized situations, or as normal as they could be in Berlin, a taut, anxious city."

"Heroes" was released on October 14, 1977, and was promptly described by one enthusiast as: "An astounding piece of work, an act of courage." Bowie rejected any complaints that it lacked the humanity of his earlier rock albums. "Personally, in private, I've never been interested in rock. I listen to it only in an analytical way, in search of ideas. I don't get great pleasure from it. That's finished."

The gloom of Berlin extended beyond the shores of Germany. It was as if a strange pall of darkness had fallen over Bowie at this time, a black cloud that seemed to pursue him and enshroud all those who came near him. Death and tragedy were not far away, even at the very point when it seemed he was beginning to lighten up and make some effort to return to the material world of touring and public appearances.

In September, 1977, Bowie was reunited with his old friend Marc Bolan for a guest appearance on his new TV series, *Marc*. Intended as a show for children, the series was hosted by Bolan, who was relishing his comeback role after some years in the wilderness following the end of his T Rex chart success. His guests on the show, recorded at Granada TV's Manchester studios, also included new punk heroes Generation X and pub rockers Eddie and The Hot Rods (who, incidentally, never got to perform).

A trainload of music press reporters were invited to attend the filming and found themselves being chased around the studio by Bowie's singularly unpleasant minder. There were all sorts of ructions in the studio, including a row between Generation X and their manager and the producer. Bolan was thrilled by the presence of his old rival in the studio and was desperately looking forward to singing a couple of numbers with him. Bowie sang '"Heroes'", and when Bowie and Bolan finally got on the small podium together, under the harsh studio lights, they struck up with an improvised tune called 'Standing Next To You'. Bowie was a little alarmed and not best pleased to find that Bolan's backing band included Herbie Flowers and Tony Newman, both veterans of the *Diamond Dogs* Tour that had resulted in a backstage row. However, Bowie carried on, looking increasingly bemused, but smiling at Bolan's eagerness to please.

Then Bowie got an electric shock from the microphone and Bolan actually fell off the stage in his excitement. He was not drunk, as has sometimes been claimed. I was in the studio at the time and chatted to Bolan just a few minutes before his big moment. He simply wanted was to create the best show of the series that was proudly called *Marc*. But there had been so much delay leading up to the big moment, that the electricians refused to work overtime and "pulled the plugs" at 7pm, just as the pair were getting into the number. You could see the scowling contempt on the faces of the union men who once controlled British TV with an iron hand. Fortunately, enough of the run through had been recorded for it to be salvaged for an edited version to be shown later. Bowie had returned to Berlin when he received the tragic news. Just a week after the TV session, on September 16, 1977, Marc Bolan, the creator of T Rex and the Glam Rock boom, was killed in a car crash on Barnes Common, London. Bowie, who had just recorded a few demos with Bolan and planned further collaborations, was devastated. He attended the funeral, held at Golders Green Crematorium on September 20, 1977, and went into mourning. He set up a trust fund for Bolan's son Rolan and, at the same time, took stock of his own life, returning to visit his childhood homes in London in an understandable fit of nostalgia and deep sorrow.

But life goes on. Bowie had undertaken a most unexpected project at this time, which couldn't have been further removed from his work with Eno. He was invited to sing a duet with the famous American crooner and movie actor Bing Crosby. The star of the famous "*Road*" movies with Bob Hope, the man who had sung 'White Christmas' – arguably the biggest pop hit of all time – was teamed up with the erstwhile Ziggy Stardust and the man who played the koto on 'Moss Garden'. In fact, it was not *such* an unlikely pairing, given

Bowie's theatrical and movie background, and his proven ability to sing in a straight ballad style. In later years Frank Sinatra would team up on records with latter-day pop idols, including Bono of U2. But Bing 'n' Bowie did it first. The choice of material was nothing like 'Queen Bitch' or 'Width Of A Circle' but closer in spirit to 'True Love'. When Bowie guested on the Bing Crosby's *Merrie Olde Christmas* TV show, filmed in London, the odd couple, clad in identical smart blazers, sang a duet on 'The Little Drummer Boy'. Crosby complimented Bowie on his singing and asked for his home phone number, but the black cloud loomed and Crosby died just a month later. In a further odd twist, this unique performance with Bowie became a hit record five years later, when 'Peace On Earth – Little Drummer Boy' reached Number 3 in the UK charts in December, 1982.

Another unlikely scenario flowed. In February, 1978, Bowie was busy in Berlin filming *Just A Gigolo*, which featured legendary actress Marlene Dietrich. Comically bad, with wooden acting and a dismal story line, the film was given a hostile critical reception when shown at the Cannes Film festival.

Eventually Bowie stopped messing about and got back to work. On March 29 he began his 1978 World Tour, which opened in San Diego, USA with Carlos Alomar playing rhythm guitar and hastily-recruited Adrian Belew on lead. He also performed a 13-week British tour set beginning in June.

Following the success of *"Heroes"*, another Bowie studio album was not scheduled until *Lodger* was issued in 1979. In the meantime, Bowie's recording commitments were met by releasing a double live set called *Stage*, complementing his 1974's *David Live*. Like its predecessor, it was recorded in Philadelphia, this time at The Spectrum, and comprised an action-packed series of performances from the shows on April 28-29, 1978.

On tour, Bowie was prepared to mix both old and new material, meeting fans half-way by giving rousing performances of old favourites like 'Ziggy Stardust' (complete with long-drawn-out cry of "and Ziggy played guitar!") while introducing the more advanced ideas from *Low* and *"Heroes"*. For example, cuts like 'Five Years', 'Soul Love', 'Star', and 'Station To Station' were intermingled with 'Warszawa', 'Art Decade', and a Mellotron-laden 'Sense Of Doubt'. Adrian Belew played the old Mick Ronson riffs of the Ziggy era and coped with 'Breaking Glass' and 'Beauty And The Beast'. Roger Powell played keyboards and synthesizers instead of Eno, and Bowie's most experienced men, Carlos Alomar and Dennis Davis, kept the continuity flowing.

The 17 tracks were put into a different sequence from the actual show by producer Tony Visconti and, although you can hear the audience cheering, they are kept pretty much in the background and there is generally more of a studio

"I SUPPOSE IT'S NOT THE HAPPIEST OF ALBUMS BUT IT WASN'T ALL SUBJECTIVE. IT WAS TAKEN FROM OBSERVATIONS."
DAVID BOWIE

than a live feel about proceedings. *Stage* was released on September 25, 1978, and was felt to be much better than *David Live*, although Bowie, himself, had some pretty disparaging things to say about rock music and touring during his press and TV interviews at the time. It seemed he still carried a deep bitterness over the way he was treated during his greatest rock success.

Bowie's disenchantment with the music business and with rock was a bad reaction to being ripped off. As a young Mod he loved the bands he had paid tribute to on *Pin Ups* with such energy and affection. But then image and the theatre of fame has always been more interesting to him than the nuts and bolts of rock 'n' roll. Better to sit in a Japanese moss garden practising the koto than bashing out 'Fame' at the Ipswich Gaumont any day. "I don't think there is a real life for a rock artist," he told one reporter in June, 1978. "It's hanging on to a shallow means of livelihood. I wouldn't give that position to anybody if it were in my power." He revealed just how badly he been bruised by his post-Ziggy experiences when he said: "I seriously thought I was coming to the end of my tether. I considered everything as a way out – even suicide." Heard in the light of that grim statement, the music of *"Heroes"* makes a lot more sense.

BEAUTY AND THE BEAST

Beauty And The Beast is a story of great antiquity. It tells the tale of a handsome woman with an uncouth male companion. They are the hero and heroine of the well-known fairy tale in which Beauty saves the life of her father by consenting to live with The Beast. In the ensuing relationship, The Beast becomes enchanted and as a result turns into a handsome prince and marries the girl.

This opening salvo from the album contains suitably Beastly noises created by some sort of electronic device, which sounds like *The Elephant Man* with a bad head cold. From the outset it is clear that Bowie intended to be much more vocally involved on this side of the album, abandoning the restraint shown during the making of *Low*. "You can't say no to The Beauty And The Beast", he chants in a rather menacing tone. The whole piece is full of menace and aggression and sustains the dark and brooding atmosphere that pervades the album. "I wanted to believe me, I wanted to be good," sings Bowie, hinting at conversations with himself about his personal life and in possible reference to his half-brother. In the tradition of the best poets, none of this is revealed too clearly for fear of appearing bland, simplistic and matter-of-fact. Bowie implies that both ugliness and beauty have their own place in the scheme of things and can be equally important. Many Bowie aficionados will recall the feeling of shock when they first heard this intense, hypnotic performance, during which the anachronistic chaos of modern pop music was created, at a stroke. 'Beauty And The Beast' was released as a single, coupled with 'Sense Of Doubt', in January, 1978, but only got as far as Number 39 in the UK charts. (Incidentally, this album was the first to include a lyric sheet since *Aladdin Sane*, hinting at Bowie's renewed confidence as a writer.)

JOE THE LION

Bowie spent quite a lot of time on his own in Berlin and sought company and solace in various bars, including Joe's Beer House, which at times proved a rather dispiriting experience. He'd sometimes get quite aggressive and miserable and he saw the same effect in others. 'Joe The Lion' goes to the bar demanding "d-r-i-n-k-s on the house" and plans to buy a gun, once he's got sufficient Dutch courage. Said Bowie: "Berlin is a city made up of bars for sad, disillusioned people to get drunk in. I've taken full advantage of working there to examine the place intensively." However, it seems that the story of Joe The Lion was inspired, not so much by a rather grim night on the town, as by the exploits of American performance artist Chris Burden. He would indulge in such exploits as being put into a bag over a freeway and, even as Bowie sings, of being nailed to a car. Burden was also famed for sleeping in an art gallery and for using gold nails in works of performance art that involved crucifixion. Strange behaviour, but it clearly intrigued Bowie, whose whole life had been a kind of performance art spectacular. David refers to Joe as a "fortune teller" in this dream-like narrative epic, rich in expressive phrases like "It's Monday, you slither down the greasy pipe". He also positively shouts "you get up and sleep", indicating that Berlin itself has become a kind of dreamworld inhabited by such strange creatures as Joe The Lion.

"HEROES"

Bowie claimed the song was inspired by events he spied during recording sessions at Hansa. Each day he spotted two 20-year-olds meeting at the Wall under the shadow of a gun turret. "They were obviously having an affair of some kind. There were much better places to meet, so why did they choose a

gun turret? I assumed their motive was guilt and this was an act of heroism."
Bowie admitted this could all have been the result of his imagination working
overtime – probably the two kids worked in nearby offices – but it was an
inspirational scene. Sang Bowie: "I will be king and you, you will be queen.
Though nothing will drive them away we can beat them just for one day. We
can be heroes just for one day." The song goes on to describe the scene where
the couple stand by the wall with the guns shooting above their heads as they
press lips together in the rain for a lingering kiss. Says Bowie: "The title track
of *"Heroes"* is about facing reality and standing up to it." Strangely enough
there is a suggestion by other eyewitnesses that the boy involved in the affair
was actually the 30-year-old Bowie himself. The use of quotation marks around
the title meant that Bowie felt there was something ironic about being a rock
'n' roll hero to his fans, while he kept his own emotional life as far distant and
remote and private as possible. The song was recorded in English, French and
German versions. While not a standout on the album, it got to Number 24 in
the UK chart and the song later became one of Bowie's best-known anthems
which he went on to perform memorably at *Live Aid* in 1985.

SONS OF THE SILENT AGE

The vocalist returns to the fray and revives memories of the *chanteur* of
yesteryear. Bowie sings with such power on 'Sons of the Silent Age' that it
must have alarmed his fellow musicians in the studio, grown used to the
mumbling muttering of *Low*. Some thought this mildly interesting performance
was intended as an urgent message to the blank generation of punk rockers:
get some purpose in your lives kids! Others took a different view and saw it
as a commentary on the under-educated, over-fed commuters seen standing
on railway station platforms, heading to work with "blank looks and no
books". In this scenario the sons of the silent age become middle-aged men
sleeping their way though life, and leading an existence so pointless that even
death is a footnote of no consequence. A song for the hopeless indeed.

BLACKOUT

The official line was that this was about the great blackout in the Seventies
when New York City was plunged into darkness owing to a massive power
failure. Bowie imagined a city gone mad, a time of muggings, murder and

mayhem, when "peoploids" with red eyes roamed the streets in search of victims. It was a seductive image. Even the great jazz vibraharp player, Lionel Hampton, was sufficiently inspired by that same event to produce an album called *Black Out*. In reality, most of Manhattan's population just went quietly to bed when the lights went out and nine months later there was a baby boom.

Meanwhile, back in his own life, Bowie suffered a physical blackout in Berlin when he received a surprise visit by his bubbly wife Angela, hotfoot from Switzerland. He gasped for breath and had to be rushed to a British Military hospital. At first it was feared he had a heart attack but it was diagnosed as nothing more than a panic attack. Sings Bowie in fearful tones: "Get me to a doctor's! I've been told someone's back in town, the chips are down." Later he implores "Get me some protection!" which doesn't sound much like a song about electrical power failure.

V-2 SCHNEIDER

V-2 Schneider' is a combination of influences and ideas. There is Florian Schneider of Kraftwerk, and of course the V-2 rocket bomb. Florian was the keyboard player and vocalist who worked diligently alongside Ralf Hutter in Kraftwerk, a Dusseldorf-based band that worked at Connie Plank's studios. They specialized in using experimental electronic sounds and had a hit with 'Autobahn' in both the US and UK. Bowie grew quite friendly with Florian and liked his dry sense of humour. "I like Kraftwerk as people very much and Florian in particular," said Bowie in one of his frequent public pronouncements. The V-2 was the second revenge weapon that Hitler unleashed on the Allies

A V2 ROCKET BOMB AIMED AT LONDON, 1945.

in the final days of the war. The rain of missiles was aimed mainly at London and Norwich although some were fired at Dutch cities as well, causing panic, death and destruction. It was German rocket technology that laid the foundations for the US space programme, and the V-2 was undoubtedly a symbol of power and speed. Curiously enough, this sax-laden performance sounds more like Roy Wood's band Wizzard than Kraftwerk, given its poppy treatment and relatively light-hearted theme. Bowie messes up the intro by coming in on the wrong beat and then sings, *sotto voce*, the phrase "V-2 Schneider" over a soulful bass line somewhat similar to that used on 'Rescue Me' by Fontella Bass.

SENSE OF DOUBT

This brave piece of imaginative work is best heard with a clear head and a strong stomach. The recommended time for listening is around 10am on a bright Spring morning. Heard just before going to bed on a stormy winter's night, 'Sense of Doubt' could induce nightmares and a long-term bout of depression. Four heavy left-hand notes on the piano set the scene. There is an electronic sea rustling, and a rushing wind heard in a world of Stygian darkness. Said Bowie: "Living in Berlin makes me feel uneasy, very claustrophobic. I work best under these sort of conditions." You feel the walls closing in and sense the glare of border guards, the pointing of machine guns and the distant yapping of dogs. At any moment you expect to be asked for your papers and proof of your identity, before being carted off to face a magistrate on unspecified charges. Kafkaesque indeed. The synthesizer is used to excellent effect, and there are curious, unidentified noises off as if an intruder is breaking into the conservatory. Eventually it moves into the next piece with all the stealth of a Ninja warrior seeking to murder a sleeping Emperor, and Germanic influence gives way to the land of the Rising Sun. 'Sense Of Doubt' made a strange B-side to 'Beauty And The Beast' but it gave casual listeners who bought the single a jolt.

MOSS GARDEN

Time hangs still in a moss garden, and this evocative instrumental piece moves slowly as it creates an air of peace at odds with an underlying hint of menace. Bowie makes effective use of the koto, a Japanese stringed instrument consisting of a rectangular wooden body over which are stretched 13 silk strings, usually plucked with plectra or a nail-like device. It may be that, given the somewhat furtive and uncertain playing style Bowie adopts, he was using the nail rather than a plectrum. More experienced koto players can get up quite a head of steam, playing with all the vigour of George Formby on the ukulele during his noted rendition of 'Tiger Rag'. The ukulele is a less sensitive instrument than the koto, which is at its best when used to produce the kind of anguished and spiritual tones required here. One note on the koto is worth a thousand words. The koto is one of the chief instruments in Japanese traditional music and Bowie may have been influenced by the example of Yatsuhashi Kengyo (1614-1685), who first developed the koto as a solo voice.

Moss tends to grow in dense mats on trees, rocks and moist ground. Used extensively in Japanese gardens since AD618, it induces feelings of calm conducive to contemplation and meditation. A good example of a moss garden may be found at Kokedera, The Moss Temple in Kyoto.

NEUKOLN

From Japan we set sail for Germany and arrive back in Berlin and the Turkish quarter of Neukoln. Explained Bowie: "I did a series of paintings while I was there of the Turks that live in the city. 'Neukoln' is the area of Berlin where the Turks are shackled in very bad conditions. They're very much an isolated community. It's sad. And that kind of reality obviously contributed to the mood of both *Low* and '*Heroes*.'"

Unfortunately for the poor Turks, they not only have to endure oppression and poor housing conditions but also the sound of their young English neighbour practising the saxophone by night. In the hands of a master like Johnny Hodges or Benny Carter, the alto sax is a beautiful instrument. Bowie forestalls criticism by saying: "I can't technically play the saxophone. It's the sound that matters." The tone of his saxophone here becomes increasingly like the strangled hooting of the Woolwich Ferry foghorn echoing across the River Thames – generally agreed to be one of the most unnerving sounds known to man. In discussing the use of performance art, Vivian Stanshall of the Bonzo Dog Doo Dah Band once suggested it would be interesting to record the sound of a steam roller running over one of his precious tubas. Bowie seems to have achieved that very sound here without the use of mechanized steam power.

"I SERIOUSLY THOUGHT I WAS COMING TO THE END OF MY TETHER. I CONSIDERED EVERYTHING AS A WAY OUT – EVEN SUICIDE."
DAVID BOWIE

THE SECRET LIFE OF ARABIA

Japan and Germany are suddenly jettisoned as sources of inspiration in favour of Arabia. The album concludes with the whole band brought back into play on a number that sounds oddly like 'Hit Me With Your Rhythm Stick' by Ian Dury and The Blockheads. It was obviously a popular bass riff around the studios in the late Seventies. After the mysteries and intensities of 'Moss Garden' and 'Neukoln', this light-hearted and apparently pointless ditty seems positively banal and quite incongruous. Yet some have claimed 'The Secret Life Of Arabia' is the best song on the album. Perhaps Bowie was inspired by the sight of Neukoln's Turkish women in yashmaks going about their business and began to imagine their forebears back home in Arabia travelling across the desert in search of dates, water and fresh camels. "You must see the movie the sand in my eyes, I walk through a desert song when the heroine dies," he sings, reducing everyday life once more to a scene from a movie. Tony Visconti and Antonia Maass provided backing vocals.

153

Two bonus tracks were added to the 1991 CD version, 'Abdulmajid' with an Eastern theme and a remix of 'Joe The Lion'.

Given the blend of national influences that ebb and flow throughout *"Heroes"* it was interesting to see which way he would finally turn and where his wanderlust would take him. In December, 1978, David Bowie spent Christmas in Japan.

"GROOVY BABY!" BOWIE'S SENSUAL SEMAPHORE.

LODGER

Released	May 1979
Produced by	David Bowie And Tony Visconti
Recorded at	Recorded at Mountain Studios, Montreaux, Switzerland
Musicians	David Bowie (vocals, keyboards, guitars, saxophone, koto, background vocals)
	Carlos Alomar (rhythm guitar)
	Dennis Davis (drums, percussion)
	George Murray (bass)
	Brian Eno (synthesizers, keyboards, guitar treatments)
	Robert Fripp (lead guitar)
	Tony Visconti (mandolin, backing vocals)
	Simon House (mandolin, electric violin)
	Adrian Belew (mandolin)
	Antonia Maass (backing vocals)

FANTASTIC VOYAGE

AFRICAN NIGHT FLIGHT

MOVE ON

YASSASSIN

RED SAILS

DJ

LOOK BACK IN ANGER

BOYS KEEP SWINGING

REPETITION

RED MONEY

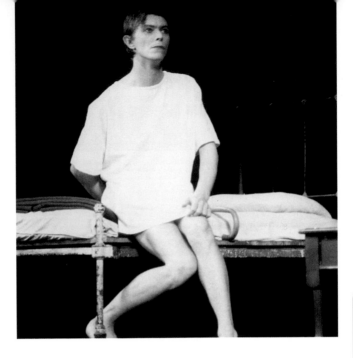

DAVID IN *THE ELEPHANT MAN* ON BROADWAY, SEPTEMBER, 1980.

Lodger might well have been called *Cuckoo*. It is an odd, slightly dotty bird that settles uneasily in the nest of Bowie albums.

It completes the so-called "Berlin Triptych", but has far less to do with the influence of the German capital or Bowie's collaboration with Eno than either *Low* or *"Heroes"*. The album was made at a time when Bowie was travelling extensively round the world and the songs reflect influences and impressions picked up on a voyage of discovery to exotic foreign lands. There were few obvious hit songs, apart from 'Boys Keep Swinging', and when one lesser-known track was released as a single, it flopped. As the end of the decade approached, Bowie was facing competition from punk rockers and new romantics. There were also fresh stars in the firmament – Elvis Costello, Sting and Gary Numan. Bowie was now an elder statesman of pop, a revered father-figure from yesteryear rather than the daring young innovator whose rightful place was at the top of the charts. But that was a situation he intended to rectify with his next dazzling album. In the meantime the world was left to puzzle over the case of the mysterious *Lodger*.

Even though his World Tour of 1978 was over (it finished in Australia in November), and it seemed he had only one hit single up his sleeve, 1979 was a remarkably busy time for Bowie. He kept on the move and there were important goings-on behind the scenes. A careful eye was kept on his business interests and there were technical developments that attracted his attention.

He had been routinely filming his shows in black and white during the previous few years. Now, with the advent of colour video technology, he was in his element. He made three promo videos for Lodger even before the MTV network came on stream, another example of his far-sighted policies.

The videos (actually shot on film) were for the three most important of the new album cuts: 'Boys Keep Swinging', 'DJ', and 'Look Back In Anger'. All three were made with top director David Mallet, who regularly worked at the helm of *The Kenny Everett Video Show*, a popular UK TV comedy series. For 'Boys Keep Swinging' Bowie popped up in drag, playing each of the three female backing singers, a surprise kept from the viewer until the end of the sequence, when one of the girls winks at the camera. Clad in a greeny-blue flared polka dot dress and a black wig, the first silly minx slinks down the catwalk then whips off her wig and smears her lipstick like an old tart. The second girl is also Bowie, dressed this time as Lauren Bacall with blonde hair and a gold lame gown. The last woman hobbles along with a stick and wears a woolly cardigan as she blows a kiss goodnight.

Bowie guested on Kenny Everett's show in April, performing 'Boys Keep Swinging'. Coupled with 'Fantastic Voyage', it was released as a single that month, and eventually got to Number 7 in the UK charts in June, 1979. When the video was later screened on prime-time TV, analysis showed that it actually had a detrimental effect on sales of the single.

It was curious that Bowie should return to androgynous Ziggy-style sensationalism for this song, having spent the last few years trying to establish himself as a serious artist working in the avant garde music field, under the tutelage of Eno. It was almost as if, on a whim, he had decided to ditch the paraphernalia of kotos and synthesizers and get back to some good old glitter rock. This alone threw in doubt the serious intent behind *Lodger*. Changes one had learned to accept and admire, yet somehow this *volte face* meant that none of his new stuff rang true, whether it was half-hearted attempts at Village People camp, or fumbling explorations into World Music. The biggest problem, however, was that all but the most loyal fans tended to react badly to the new material. They had been there with him for 'Moss Garden' and hung on desperately during 'Neukoln'. Now, with the advent of tunes like 'African Night Flight' and 'Yassassin', they had begun to lose patience. Worse still, they had begun to suspend their belief.

During an interview in New York, Bowie reiterated that he had always been interested in making neo-avant garde records and had relied on Brian Eno to help him make his own brand of experimental music. He had taken a risk in losing those fans who had first latched on to him during his successful

Young Americans period, but it was a calculated risk he was prepared to take in the interests of artistic integrity. "It started off as an experiment but I can see it continuing as long as the initial spark of excitement continues." If this were true then the conclusion to be drawn from *Lodger* was that the spark had gone out. However, it was not for want of trying to blow some heat into the creative process. Some critics were impressed by the efforts made on 'Yassassin' and 'African Night Flight', and saw them as early attempts at promoting the fusion of rock with World Music. It was an idea he could have pursued further. Said Bowie: "I never took what would be called world beat to its fruition. Brian Eno did. I think some of what we wrote together like 'African Night Flight' probably gave him the impetus to get on with things like 'My Life In The Bush Of Ghosts', which followed on from *Lodger*. He found the idea of combining different ethnic music against a Westernized beat fairly stimulating. He wanted to go with a lot of them and I didn't. But he thought what I was trying to do on those few tracks was pretty exciting."

Work began on the new album at Mountain Studios in Montreux, during a break in touring in July, 1978. Bowie recorded the fresh material with the aid of Eno and producer Tony Visconti. Among the musicians contributing were Carlos Alomar, Dennis Davis and George Murray, together with Sean Mayes on piano. Work continued into September and mixing and matching was done at the Record Plant Studios, New York. By the time the record was released, Bowie had actually moved out of his Berlin flat and he spent much more time living in a loft apartment in New York, a city that now seemed more attractive as the local artistic community expanded its activities.

Bowie's years of exile in Berlin helped him recover his sense of identity as well as his health and good spirits. He was now ready to cope with America, and the hurly-burly of everyday life, knowing he had his home in Switzerland (as well as homes at other selected world beauty spots) as a retreat if things got too rough out there on the streets.

The title *Lodger* was probably inspired by the Roman Polanski film *The Tenant*, or the first Alfred Hitchcock movie made in 1926 called *The Lodger*, although, in a sense, Bowie had always been a lodger, from his childhood in Brixton and Bromley to his days in Berlin. Although any new Bowie product was made welcome and given respectful attention, *Lodger* was disadvantaged from the outset by one of the least attractive of all his album covers. The lower part of the original LP design depicted a postcard addressed to "David Bowie c/o RCA Records" giving their London address and sent from the Lodger. The songs on the album, therefore, become postcards sent from different parts of the world with their different greetings and messages.

This was a reasonable idea. But the full-length gatefold picture of Bowie showed him apparently punched out by an assailant in a bathroom, pushed up against a wall, with his nose bent out of shape and arms, hands and legs in painful positions. As usual there was hot debate over the meaning of every nuance. Some thought the figure of the lodger represented a boyfriend who had been kicked out after an argument. This gossip may have been started to boost the old I'm-gay-and-always-have-been image. The other theory was that the artiste Bowie was not just the lodger in the flat upstairs but a lonely figure on the international stage tormented by the demands of modern society and hounded in his role as pop icon. It was stressful, but... it was a living.

It was also suggested that the beaten-up youth seen on the inside of the sleeve was lying on a mortuary slab, with his suit still on. Other disturbing images showed victims of torture and interrogation laid out for inspection, including Che Guevara just after he had been shot, Bowie being made up for the photo shoot, a baby and a familiar figure with nail holes in his hands and feet. For an album that contained many lightweight songs, this could be construed as so much tasteless blasphemy.

Before the album was released, desperate rumours were generated that, after the disappointments of *Low* and the weirdness of *Heroes*, this would be Bowie's blockbusting concept album to match The Beatles' *Sgt Pepper*. Music journalists were duly told the story behind the lodger. He was a homeless wanderer "shunned and victimized by life's pressures and technology".

When the album was eventually released in May, 1979, it was difficult to spot much in the way of a conceptualized storyline. It sounded more like a ragbag of leftover songs with references to past works and old ideas. The fact that it consisted of the best items available from some 22 tracks that Bowie and Eno had put together was not encouraging. However, there was an element of narrative in the songs, and the mood generally concerned travel and the search for identity. Interesting, but not exactly a rock opera.

However, thanks to the promo videos and the legendary name of David Bowie, the album peaked at Number 4 in the UK charts and got to Number 20 in the US. This time, Bowie did a fair amount of publicity for the album, travelling in the two months before its release from Switzerland to London, New York and even back to Australia. This was in addition to his private wanderings to Cambodia and Japan in search of Buddhist culture. Yet, relatively speaking, sales of *Lodger* proved lower than *Low* and, according to some estimates, peaked around the 140,000 mark.

During 1979, Bowie spent more time travelling, but spent less time doing interviews or giving live performances. With the advent of promo videos, there was no need for the kind of heavy in-person promotion that had become a way of life and proved so exhausting during the distant heyday of *Aladdin Sane*. The boy in the red underwear and painted face had become the businessman in a safari suit, visiting Kenya, Australia and America.

While spending time in New York at Christmas, Bowie went to see the Broadway production of *The Elephant Man* – it was a turning point in his career. He met the director and it turned out he needed a new actor to replace Philip Anglim, who was due to leave the play. Bowie was invited to take the part on the strength of his performance in *The Man Who Fell To Earth*.

Bowie gave it some thought and finally agreed to take on the difficult task of portraying the life of deformed John Merrick, the real-life Elephant Man of Victorian England. He spent a lot of time researching the subject and subsequently gave a critically-acclaimed series of performances in the role, commencing with a short season in Denver, Colorado on July 29, 1980. The play broke box office records and later moved to Chicago for a further three weeks during August. The role elevated Bowie's prestige and gave him a glimpse of a real future as an all-round artist working in many different areas. He needn't be tied to making albums like *Lodger* if he lacked inspiration in future. He could be an actor, a painter, a man for all seasons, or a "generalist" as he preferred. The strange thing was, that once he received that boost to his pride and reputation, his music also began to improve.

In Bowie's private life too, things were looking better all the time. At the beginning of the year it was announced that his divorce from Angela Bowie was finalized. As part of the settlement he formally gained custody of their son Joe, who had been living and travelling with him ever since the bust-up in Berlin two years earlier. He only had a couple more years to run with his RCA and Mainman contracts.

FANTASTIC VOYAGE

Literate lyrics set the retrospective mood of the album on which Bowie avows that dignity is valuable and that "our lives are valuable too". He is clearly distancing himself, with the benefit of hindsight, from the undignified madness of his rock 'n' roll youth. However, the somewhat lugubrious tone and vocal mannerisms he employs on 'Fantastic Voyage' tend to produce a smile rather than expressions of compassion and understanding. Only the most earnest students of Bowie would find this bland pop song more than a disappointment. Bowie sings like the male romantic lead in a Thirties musical comedy, and is answered by the boys in the chorus chanting "it's a moving world". It's a strangely old-fashioned format, heightened by the use of backing mandolins played by Tony Visconti, Simon House and Adrian Belew. Curiously at odds with the inconsequential nature of the melody are such faintly political statements as: "That's no reason to shoot some of those missiles". The unnecessary repetition of "We're learning to live with somebody's depression and I don't want to live with somebody's depression" is sufficiently gauche to cause pursed lips and tut-tuts from anyone concerned with preserving the art of writing popular songs. The line doesn't have the ring of, say, "In a mountain greenery, where God paints the scenery".

To be fair, the lyricist is attempting to convey some heavy thoughts about our political leaders and the on-going (Seventies) threat of a nuclear holocaust. Bowie talked about the album when it was released in rather more depth than he did about more interesting previous albums. "It's a pretty straightforward song about how I feel in a very old-fashioned romantic

AUTHOR CHRISTOPHER ISHERWOOD (LEFT) AND POET W. H. AUDEN (RIGHT) TAKE A TRAIN TO CHINA IN 1938.

fashion. One feels constantly that so many things are out of our own control and it's just this infuriating thing that you don't want to have their depression ruling your life or dictating how you will wake up each morning."

During the construction of 'Fantastic Voyage' the band played the same chord sequence four different ways. Bowie explained: "The same thing occurs elsewhere on the album. I wanted to put a point of view forward in a narrative fashion right at the front of the album." The chord sequence crops up again on the eighth track, 'Boys Keep Swinging'. Strangely enough, the whole piece also sounds strongly related to 'Word On A Wing' from the 1976 album *Station to Station* – same tempo, same groove. Eno's main contribution to this piece would appear to be an ambient drone, although this is hard to detect.

AFRICAN NIGHT FLIGHT

Bowie had spent several safari holidays in Africa, communing with the natives, and this was the setting for one of his most curious confections. Spooky jungle noises abound and are described on the sleeve credits as "cricket menace", attributed to the redoubtable Eno and his ingenious synthesizer. Opinions vary as to the merits of this controversial 'Night Flight'. Some have described it as the most innovative work on the album. Others see it as derivative and self-indulgent as Bowie prattles through the densely-packed lyrics in a jumbled parody of 'Night Mail'. This celebrated poem, by W. H. Auden, was from a 1936 documentary film about the railway postal delivery system. At the time it was a ground-breaking idea to make a film about real workers and to blend poetry with fast-moving images. Wystan Hugh Auden (1907–73) was a friend of Christopher Isherwood (of Berlin fame) and they travelled the world together writing about international social problems, including Japanese aggression in China. Top British national newspaper columnist Jean Rook, writing in *The Daily Express*, generously thought of Bowie as a modern-day rock poet and stated, in a revealing interview, that he was: "The nearest thing to Christopher Isherwood, whom Bowie idolizes."

In the middle of Bowie's Auden-inspired verse comes the use of the Swahili phrase "Asanti habari... Asanti nabana" which apparently means "Hello and Goodbye". The inspiration came from Bowie's trip to Mombasa, Kenya: "I'd spent a month and a half in Kenya before I wrote 'African Night Flight' and once I got there I'd taken, not night flights, but a number of afternoon flights with a guide called Mrs Sutherland. She had a pair of horn-rimmed glasses, a long cigarette-holder, and she was continually losing her flight map."

Bowie boarded a four-seater plane and went off into Masai territory to look out for rhino and giraffes: "I found that terribly exciting and it was the impetus for the song." Apart from wild beasts of the jungle, Bowie also discovered a lost tribe of German pilots, still wearing their flying gear. These relics of World War II fascinated Bowie. "You've got a good idea why they are there in the first place, but they live strange lives flying about in their Cessnas over the bush land doing all kinds of strange things. They're very mysterious characters, permanently plastered and always talking about when they are going to leave. The song came about because I was wondering exactly what they were doing there and why they flew around."

Bowie sings in rapid bursts of Zen-inspired prose: "Over the bush land over the trees wise like orangutan that was me." Stranger still is the composer's suggestion that the track is based on the chords of 'Suzie Q', a song recorded by Dale Hawkins in 1957 and again by Credence Clearwater Revival in 1968. Said Bowie: "We took the basic idea of 'Suzie Q' and played it backwards. Then Brian decided to put prepared piano on it. He put pairs of scissors and all kinds of metal things on the strings of the piano." This was added to obtain the kind of ragtime sound that popular Fifties entertainer Winifred Atwell used on what she proudly called "my other piano". (Incidentally she used drawing pins, not scissors.) So 'African Night Flight' takes us from Auden to Atwell via the Luftwaffe. Bowie was nothing if not eclectic.

MOVE ON

Moving on in the whirlwind flight around the World, country star Johnny Cash seems to be the vocal inspiration for 'Move On'. Here Bowie completes a hat trick; three less-than-satisfying songs in a row. With its thundering hooves and cowboy-style vocals, this is pure pastiche; this is Bowie, master of the wind-up. At least the lyrics are clearly defined and require no soul-searching for hidden meanings. "Sometimes I feel that I need to move on, so I pack a bag and move on," sings Bowie boldly and firmly. Goodbye Nietzsche and hello *Which? Holiday Guide*.

As he sets sail at dawn, the destinations are clearly mapped out. Africa (full of sleepy people), Russia (with its horsemen), Cyprus too (former home of Angie Bowie) – all places where he might meet the girl of his dreams. With a fair wind and a packed lunch there's no telling how far he might go. Bowie, in his discussions about the album, described 'Move On' as "blatantly romantic".

The middle section came about as a result of happy chance. While playing through some old tapes on a Revox machine, he accidentally twisted some tape and played it backwards. He thought the resulting mesh of strange sounds were quite beautiful. "Without listening to what it was originally we recorded the whole thing note for note backwards and then I added vocal harmonies with Tony Visconti." He added that playing this section backwards again would reveal the true source – a version of 'All The Young Dudes'. "I did this in New York, which was very exciting. I was so pleased that the conclusion of these three albums was so 'up'. You never know until you come out of the studio exactly what you've done and it would have been terribly depressing if the third one had been down. At least this one has a kind of optimism." This track also underlined the kind of production techniques employed by Bowie, Eno and Visconti. Clearly a humdinger of an "oblique strategy", the backwards message also hints at magical practice.

YASSASSIN

The title is Turkish for "Long Live". Rock 'n' roll may have been guilty of many sins during its ascendance, but none so strange as this excursion into World Music. It features the wailing of a violin and is set to a lilting Jamaican-cum-Eastern rhythm that introduces the sumptuous world of the West Indian kebab house. Bowie sings "I'm not a moody guy… just a working man, no judge of men." He sings of the proud, good folk who come from the farmlands to live in the city. These are not warriors. They don't want to fight, just to be left in peace.

Bowie was particularly pleased with this track as it highlights the electric violin work of Simon House, a former member of Hawkwind, who had been to school with Bowie some 15 years earlier and was delighted to receive a call inviting him to take part on the sessions. Said Bowie proudly: "He understood the notation immediately, even though he had no experience with Turkish music before. This song is about the kind of character that you find in coffee bars in Turkey. An interesting thing about this track was putting two ethnic sounds together. We used the Turkish things and put them against a Jamaican back-beat. They're both parallel."

RED SAILS

'Red Sails' sounds suspiciously like the incoherent ramblings of a lost soul. Quite apart from the dead studio sound and the weak guitar work (there are two guitarists: Carlos Alomar and Adrian Belew), the lyrics reveal the composer at a low ebb. "Feel a bit roughed, feel a bit frightened… red sail action, wake up in the wrong town," It continues in a desultory fashion before Bowie actually resorts to singing: "And it's far far far far far… da-da-da" and so on, over a childlike punk-rock rhythm and febrile guitar solo that heads nowhere. In justifying this track Bowie explained: "We took a German new music feel and put against it the idea of a contemporary English mercenary-cum-swashbuckling Errol Flynn, and put him in the China Sea. We have a lovely cross-reference of cultures. I honestly don't know what it's about." Alas, this was a cross-culture too far, extinguishing all semblance of musical identity.

DJ

One of the great shocks to the system of all rock and pop musicians during the late Seventies was the development of the DJs as a star attraction. This might have been because the new breed of club DJs gave the public what they wanted – entertaining music people could dance to and easily understand. More than could be said of certain superstars who abused their positions by churning out albums mainly designed to comply with contractual obligations, making music that claimed to be experimental but proved to be derivative and joyless. Disco, despised as a commercial and cultural blind alley, was often more inventive and democratic. It certainly wasn't elitist. Said Bowie: "This is somewhat cynical but it's my natural response to disco. The DJ is the one who is having ulcers now, not the executives, because if you do the unthinkable thing of putting a record on in a disco not in time… that's it. If you have 30 seconds silence, your whole career is over."

Bowie sang plaintively: "I am a DJ I am what I play". Marginally better than any of the self-indulgent meanderings on side one of the vinyl album, 'DJ' was blessed with a firm riff and some better bass and guitar work. Even so, there are some decidedly dodgy drums.

A special video was made to promote 'DJ' as a single, in which Bowie appeared in a pink suit, but it failed to get higher than Number 29 in the UK.

"DJ" could also stand for one David Jones. In the video Bowie, as the disc jockey, goes berserk and sprays his initials on a bathroom mirror.

LOOK BACK IN ANGER

Look Back In Anger was one of the proposed titles for the album but was later dropped. A fast gallop with overtones of Led Zeppelin's 'Achilles Last Stand', it has some whiney backing vocals from Bowie and Visconti chanting "Waiting so long" and, if you listen carefully, you can hear Eno's synthesized "horse trumpets" braying in the distance. His "Eroica horn" is more difficult to spot. The song is about the Angel of Death. Said Bowie: "I had this thought about angels and Angels of Death, which is the character that is most revered. But this one is about a tatty Angel of Death. We did one thing on this track which was a lot of fun but terribly frustrating for the musicians. Brian and I came up with a series of cards with chords on. We stuck them on a blackboard and we had all the musicians sitting on chairs in front of the blackboard. Then Brian and I just pointed at the one to play next. It got very intense and the more intense it got, the better it got. We did that for 30 minutes and kept yelling out the style to play in. Fortunately I am with guys who are very receptive to what I want to do. They get angry of course, but only if they're not fully aware of what is going on. Often I can't help them much because I'm not sure what's going to come out of it either."

All this might explain the generally poor standard of playing on the album and the lack of musical involvement at a grass-roots level. This was another *Lodger* track to inspire the creation of a special promotional video. The story line was based on Oscar Wilde's haunting story, *The Picture Of Dorian Gray*. Bowie is seen in an artist's garret, singing while admiring a self-portrait. He then turns into the Angel of Death, picking at his sores before collapsing.

'Look Back In Anger' was not released as a single in the UK, although it was issued in the US. Surprisingly, given its unmemorable content, the song was performed live, as the opening number on some of the "Serious Moonlight" shows four years later and also on the 1995 "Outside" Tour.

The title comes from the 1956 John Osborne play, which sparked the "kitchen sink" drama revolution in post-war England. For some, the lyrics hint at a regretful overview of Bowie's career so far. Of course Bowie has often stated that his songs have no real meaning at all and that he is the last person to understand them. As the late John Osborne might have said, they are "inadmissible evidence".

BOYS KEEP SWINGING

This track was the biggest hit from the album, which is rather surprising given that the marching beat is a kind of throwback to the Sixties and is more than a tad old-fashioned. Singing about "boys" in this way isn't even "camp" in a theatrical sense and sounds rather overdone.

Musically, the drumming is leaden and the guitar solo is surely one of the poorest ever committed to posterity by the electro-magnetic recording process. Even the bass playing, not normally a major problem for even the least competent rock musician, consists of a series of inexpertly-plucked drum notes. Mercifully, there is an explanation for all this. Apparently Bowie thought it would be interesting to ask the band to swap instruments – Carlos Alomar is responsible for the ham-fisted drumming and Dennis Davis attempts to play the bass. It may well be that Bowie himself is responsible for the hideous guitar solo. The idea was to create a garage band sound – but most garage bands sound a good deal better than this. When you're a boy you can wear a uniform. When you're a boy other boys check you out." The message is that boys have more fun than girls. Or they did before the advent of the Spice Girls.

Bowie explained: "What we did on this one was to have everybody play the instruments they didn't usually play. Suddenly we had Carlos Alomar, who is the rhythm guitarist, on drums and Dennis Davis on bass. What was extraordinary as the enthusiasm that came from musicians who weren't playing their usual instrument. They became kids discovering rock 'n' roll for the first me again! The tune has exactly the same chord sequence as fantastic Voyage'."

It may have seemed a good idea the studio but in the harsh light of headphones, it doesn't add up. Bowie admitted as much in a radio interview when he let slip: "That song really does have a problem."

REPETITION

'Repetition' is a merry tune about wife-beating, based on stories Bowie read in American newspapers. The guitar riff is meant to represent the repeated blows of a brutal husband beating his spouse. The hero, Johnny, is a big man who comes home after work to find that his dinner is cold. As he rains blows on his long-suffering and allegedly incompetent wife, he muses on the sorry fact that he could have married Anne with the blue silk blouse instead. "Can't you even cook? What's the use of me working when you can't damn cook?" he grumbles petulantly. It's an attempt at a dramatized documentary and works reasonably well, although when the listener's patience is exhausted by such tracks as 'African Night Flight' and 'Red Sails', even *Low* songs tend to get overlooked. Bowie sings in a completely lifeless tone that implies he doesn't much believe in the lyrics. Strangely, he seemed quite pleased with this effort and said later: "I think my voice sounded rather like it did five years ago." He admitted that much of *Lodger* contained elements of ideas that could have come from the many different eras of his career.

RED MONEY

'Red Money' and 'Repetition' both feature the synthesizer playing of Roger Powell, who came into the studio at Eno's suggestion, via Todd Rundgren's Utopia. Eno himself makes no contribution to the song, which bears more than a passing resemblance to Iggy Pop's 'Sister Midnight' from *The Idiot* (1977). According to Bowie: "This song, I think, is about responsibility. Red boxes keep cropping up in my paintings and they represent responsibility." He sings: "I was really feeling good, Reet Petite and how d'ya do, then I got the small red box and I didn't know what to do… project cancelled."

The reference to 'Reet Petite' is interesting – this was, of course, the groundbreaking hit song recorded by Jackie Wilson in 1957, part-written by Berry Gordy Jnr, who later established Motown records as a result of his songwriting success. As "red money" could mean the debit entries in a ledger, the implication is a star himself with responsibilities to the public and others, and then had to juggle with high finance as a consequence. He can't leave his responsibilities behind, having worked so hard to reach his present position, even if he'd like to fly off around the world and forget everybody. Oh, but he'd send them a postcard.

The CD version of *Lodger* contains the bonus tracks 'I Pray, Ole' and a 1988 remake of 'Look Back In Anger', with Reeves Gabrels (who would later be recruited by Bowie into Tin Machine) on guitar. After this debacle, Bowie set to work on *Scary Monsters*. Although *Lodger* was said to be the last of the Berlin Triptych, in fact Bowie continued working with many of the same musicians on his next album, including Carlos Alomar and Dennis Davis, thankfully returning to their chosen instruments. As for the triptych, Bowie later said: "I just liked the word."

SCARY MONSTERS

Released	September 1980
Produced by	David Bowie and Tony Visconti
Recorded at	Power Station, New York
Musicians	David Bowie (vocals, keyboards)
	Carlos Alomar, Chuck Hammer, Robert Fripp, Pete Townshend (guitars)
	Chuck Hammer (guitar synthesizer)
	Andy Clark (synthesizer)
	Tony Visconti (acoustic guitar, backing vocals)
	Roy Bittan (piano)
	George Murray (bass)
	Dennis Davis (percussion)
	Michi Hirota (voice)
	Lynn Maitland, Chris Porter (backing vocals)

IT'S NO GAME (PART 1)
UP THE HILL BACKWARDS
SCARY MONSTERS (AND SUPER CREEPS)
ASHES TO ASHES
FASHION
TEENAGE WILDLIFE
SCREAM LIKE A BABY
KINGDOM COME (VERLAINE)
BECAUSE YOU'RE YOUNG
IT'S NO GAME (PART 2)

A SCARY MONSTER INDEED.

When John Lennon sang that most personal of songs, 'Mother', his tormented cries struck a chord in all but the most insensitive of souls. The anguished voice calling out "Mama don't go home!", on his 1970 *John Lennon* album, expressed a great purging of his soul, an agonizing process that he shared with a vast and sympathetic audience. When David Bowie unleashed his most angry and powerful album, he too was attempting to exorcise demons that had been troubling him for years. *Scary Monsters* was an outpouring of anger and bitterness, enacted with a violent belligerence. This was in shocking contrast to the more mellifluous moods that had illuminated much of his previous work. But fans should not have been surprised. Bowie had already hinted in 'The Width Of A Circle' from *The Man Who Sold The World* that "The monster was me". Now, in his even more scary moments, Bowie was ready to set the monsters free.

Anguished howls and tortured guitars dominate proceedings on David Bowie's final album for RCA. The mood is almost uniformly bleak; there is little sign of romanticism or the twinkling humour that had palliated even his most doom-laden work, unless you count the moment when he mutters: "We are the goon squad and we're coming to town. Beep! Beep!" In fact, Bowie appears to have been in a foul temper when he recorded *Scary Monsters* – he snaps and snarls about being "insulted by fascists" and screams "Shut up!" at his lead guitarist.

It is a cry that is richly deserved as the grouchy guitar player in question matches the over-riding mood of "rock rage" with corresponding violence. Why so tetchy? At this stage in Bowie's career everything should have been hunky dory. Following the separation of 1978, David and Angela Bowie were finally divorced in February 1980. Angie received a sizeable settlement and

David gained custody of his son Joe. Bowie was approaching the end of his old record company and management contracts, which meant he could negotiate a better financial future. Thanks to his role in *The Elephant Man*, which began in July, 1980, Bowie was hailed as an accomplished actor with offers of pantomime pouring in, not to mention many serious TV plays and film roles. 'Ashes To Ashes' was released in August and became one of his biggest selling singles. A month later, the album *Scary Monsters* was released, hotly pursued by 'Fashion', another big hit in October, 1980. (Just to be a fly in the ointment, Angela Bowie published her book *Free Spirit* about her life with Bowie around this time.) Completing a good year for Bowie was the release of a K-Tel special *The Best Of David Bowie*, a welcome compilation comprising 16 great tracks including 'Life On Mars', 'Starman', and '*Young Americans*', which became a huge hit thanks to heavy TV promotion. This was the David Bowie the general public knew and loved and their support for the record was a kind of polite commentary on his output of the previous three years.

With all this success he was now, despite his protestations, becoming a very rich man. Certainly he was better off than the skinny impoverished London boy who once needed feeding with crab and sweetcorn soup to keep his strength up. Surrounded by adoring fans, feted by figures from the worlds of art and entertainment, a master of his own destiny and free to paint, make records, act in films and plays and drink the odd glass of wine among merry company of his own choosing – what better life could a fellow lead? And yet there was darkness, fury, wild mutterings. All of this emerges among the tumult and hubbub that is *Scary Monsters*.

The creator of this monstrous work explained: "*Scary Monsters* for me has always been some kind of purge. It was me eradicating the feelings within myself that I was uncomfortable with. You have to accommodate your pasts within your persona. You have to understand why you went through them. You cannot just ignore them or put them out of your mind or pretend they didn't happen or just say 'Oh I was so different then'. It's very important to get into them and understand them. It helps you reflect on what you are now."

Those bad feelings might have been an accumulation of guilt about past misdeeds, of anger at his own mistreatment at the hands of others, and perhaps that overwhelming sense of never quite knowing if he was pursuing the right path or making the right decisions. On balance it appeared that Bowie was generally right, although there were always the critics to contend with. Whatever he did there were bound to be complaints. Yet he was widely admired for his past achievements, respected for his intelligence and loved for his glamour and charm. There were few in the firmament of rock stars who could combine so many different appealing facets. There were plenty of charmless, ignorant oafs, but there was only one David Bowie. Whatever the deep reasons for his discontent, they seemed to surface on *Scary Monsters*. It didn't hurt that his new sound, rock-fuelled and angst-ridden, seemed more in tune with the aggression of the times than the experimental avant garde art music of recent memory.

Once again, Bowie's old friend Tony Visconti was called upon to act as co-producer on the project and the musicians included Carlos Alomar, Dennis Davis, George Murray, Chuck Hammer and Robert Fripp. Others taking bit parts were Roy Bittan, Andy Clark, Pete Townshend, Lynn Maitland, Chris Porter and Michi Horita, together with chief knob-twiddler Tony Visconti making his own instrumental contributions.

Sessions took place at The Power Station in New York – Bowie was staying in Greenwich Village. The backing tracks were put down first and lead guitar overdubs put on by the guest guitarists. The lyrics were written in advance, instead of being put together at the last minute or, as Bowie sometimes did, sung and improvised at the microphone during a take. The atmosphere of Manhattan and the Village, with their rich seams of streetlife characters, certainly added to the hustling mood of the album.

The new material was seen as a well-balanced advance on the achievements of *Low*, *"Heroes"* and *Lodger*, combining a degree of experimentation, shock tactics and more familiar pop melodies with a contemporary disco pulse. Although *Scary Monsters* (not forgetting the 'Super Creeps') was not a concept album in the sense of a Ziggy or *Diamond Dogs*, nevertheless there was a return to narrative themes and even hints of Bowie's beloved sci-fi. The dominant tone seemed to reflect the rumblings of discontent affecting Britain's youth in the wake of punk rock, not to mention the prevailing economic conditions back home in England and the political mood of the times. It wouldn't do for David Bowie to appear out of date or irrelevant. Singing about "kooks" or "the peoploids" might not have gone down too well with fashion-conscious Eighties people, especially when Adam Ant and Boy George were busy putting on their make-up in the dressing rooms of pop.

In a sense, *Scary Monsters* was a couple of years too late. The Sex Pistols had long since bombarded the world with Anarchy In The UK. Pete Townshend, a guest on *Scary Monsters*, had recently had a hit with 'Rough Boys', and Pink Floyd's Roger Waters was heard to grumble and grunt on *The Wall* a year before. For some music lovers it was all a grim prospect. Given the screaming vocals and raging guitars that infected the remnants of traditional rock music at this time, it seemed like all the joy had gone out of popular music. It had all been such fun when Bill Haley, Elvis and Little Richard were coming to town. Instead of providing uplifting, inspirational music, rich in humanity, the sound of 1980 seemed cold, ugly and self-obsessed. The Small Faces had once memorably sung "You can get high!" in their bouncy classic 'Itchy Coo Park'. Now it was time to come down and suffer the miseries of cold turkey, or in this case, chilled ham.

In Bowie's case you could almost sense the cold, cracked actor picking over the bones of his career. Yet many thought *Scary Monsters* was one of his best albums, and critics queued up to give it rave reviews. It was certainly his biggest seller in some years, thanks to the success of 'Fashion' and 'Ashes To Ashes'. But that didn't make it an easy listening experience. This was Bowie, the self-flagellating observer of the follies of the human race, going forth equipped to punish the rest of us. And he meant to make it hurt.

The album appeared in a distinctive cover designed by Edward Bell, with Japanese-style hand-brushed lettering and a collage of pictures and photographs showing Bowie in a pierrot's costume, designed by Natasha Komilof. The costume was an action replay of the outfit he wore in the video for 'Ashes To Ashes' and neatly gave an impression of the Bowie of yesteryear – an aesthetic, mysterious character – making a comeback. Not quite Ziggy, but close enough. One green and one blue eye peered out while a shrivelled hand held the inevitable ash-laden cigarette. On the back of the original sleeve there were references to past covers including *"Heroes", Lodger* and *Low*.

Bowie was delighted with the results of all his hard work; his decision to return to the mainstream was vindicated when he topped the British chart for only the second time in his career. 'Ashes To Ashes' got to Number 1 in the UK in the summer. Surprisingly, despite massive RCA publicity which compared it to 'Space Oddity', it was not a Top 40 hit in the US. But when *Scary Monsters (And Super Creeps)* – to give it its full title – was released, on September 12, 1980, it shot straight to Number 4 in the UK charts.

The album had been delayed in the US until Bowie had began playing his part in *The Elephant Man*, with the aim of focussing attention on both projects. The role required a huge physical effort, since he had to give the illusion of being deformed for many hours both during make-up and on stage. After his performances in Denver and Chicago, the play transferred to New York in the Autumn. It was while David was performing at the Booth Theatre that he heard the dreadful news that his old friend John Lennon had been shot dead. It was on the night of December 8, 1980. John and his wife Yoko Ono had returned home from a recording studio. As they entered the courtyard of the Dakota building, John heard a voice say "Mr Lennon" and turned around.

He was shot five times by his assailant and died shortly after from loss of blood, at the Roosevelt hospital. As the news flashed around the world, his fans were in shock. None was more shocked than David Bowie. They had not worked together since 'Fame' but they had remained mutual admirers.

Not only were Bowie and his fellow rock stars stunned by this totally pointless crime, they were understandably frightened and concerned for their own safety. Security measures were tightened up. Bowie had previously been happy to walk unaccompanied to the theatre for his show each night. He carried on and avoided the use of bodyguards, but when it was suggested that *The Elephant Man* could continue for an extended season, Bowie declined and, once the play ended its Broadway run, he left New York for a safer environment, back home in Switzerland. It later transpired that Lennon's assassin Mark Chapman had been to a performance of *The Elephant Man* at the Booth Theatre, which was about 30 blocks away from Lennon's home. At the stage door he took a picture of Bowie and even boasted to a girlfriend about what else he could have done if he hadn't shot Lennon. When Chapman's hotel room was searched, a programme was found for *The Elephant Man* with Bowie's name marked in black ink. Bowie gave his last performance as John Merrick on January 4, 1981.

In Switzerland, he kept a low profile for a year before teaming up with Queen in the chance recording session that resulted in 'Under Pressure', a highly successful hit single. It topped the UK chart in November, 1981. Bowie fans, meanwhile, were placated by the release of *Changestwobowie*, another compilation album.

In the years that lay ahead, the Bowie whirlwind blew unabated. He continued to make films, appear in plays, write songs, recruit musicians, cut albums and embark on exhausting world tours. Whatever his ratings in the charts and popularity polls or whatever his standing with the music press, he remained incredibly active and full of surprises. He even found marital bliss once he had recovered from the wounds of his first failed marriage.

During 1982 he spent a lot of time filming *The Hunger* and *Merry Christmas Mr Lawrence*, and, in March, he appeared in Bertholt Brecht's play *Baal* on BBC TV. Brecht was Germany's greatest dramatist and poet, and won the 1922 Kleist prize for his expressionist work *Baal*. Bowie won many plaudits for his performance in the TV version, which was made under conditions of great secrecy. Bowie later contributed lyrics and vocals for the theme song to Paul Schrader's movie *Cat People Putting Out Fire*. This was but small beer. His most important step came when he switched record companies from RCA to EMI America. Asked at a press conference why he'd made the change to EMI he replied: "Because I didn't like RCA... because they didn't like me! I think I released several very intelligent and important albums on RCA which they didn't seem to give much time for. *Lodger* was very much one of them, and *Low* and *'Heroes'* were the other two."

In April, 1983 he released his most exciting record in ages, the huge Number 1 disco hit 'Let's Dance' from the album of the same name, produced by Nile Rodgers and featuring Bowie's latest guitar discovery Stevie Ray Vaughan. In June, Bowie embarked on his *Serious Moonlight 83* Tour, which opened at London's Wembley Arena. Every show was sold out. His single 'China Girl' (an old song co-written with Iggy Pop) soared to Number 2 in the UK in June, despite the video being banned by the BBC for being too sexy. The tour ended in Thailand in December, 1983, and a studio LP *Tonight* followed a year later. There were many memorable moments as Bowie became the grand old trouper of the jive generation, including a duet with Mick Jagger at the 1985 Live Aid concert. Their take on the Martha and the Vandellas soul stomper 'Dancing In The Street' got to Number 1 in UK, and was a Top 10 hit in the US. There were more acting roles in movies like *Absolute Beginners* and *The Last Temptation Of Christ*. In 1987, he released a new album, *Never Let Me Down*, and kicked off the huge *Glass Spider World Tour* with his old school friend Peter Frampton on lead guitar.

Two years later, Bowie was still coming up with fresh ideas and formed Tin Machine, a raucous hard rock band in which he insisted he was just a sideman and not the leader. They made their debut in New York and released their debut albumin June 1989.

At the start of the new decade *The Sound And Vision* World Tour 1990 began in Canada accompanied by the *Sound And Vision* album (1990). The same year he met his future wife Iman Abdul Majid, a 34-year-old Somalian-born actress and model, in Los Angeles. In 1993 he released *Black Tie White Noise* and appeared at the AIDS fund-raising gala at Wembley Stadium: *A Concert For Life – The Freddie Mercury Tribute*. During 1995, Bowie signed to Virgin Records and released *Outside*, his debut album on the label. It was a UK Top 10 hit. After The *Outsiders* and a European Tour, Bowie was inducted into The Rock 'n' Roll Hall Of Fame in January, 1996. A month later he received a BRITS Award for his Outstanding Contribution To British Music.

At the ceremony he performed 'Hello Spaceboy' with the Pet Shop Boys. On January 8, 1997 he celebrated his fiftieth birthday in New York and performed the next night to 20,000 fans at Madison Square Gardens. The same month he unleashed *Earthling*, his twenty-first studio album, and later embarked on yet another world tour.

The first decade of the new millennium saw little in the way of new material although there were still tours, compilations and remastered back catalogue releases to keep his legion of fans happy. The sheer length of his active career and his business acumen now made Bowie one of the richest and most successful men in the rock universe, with a fortune only surpassed by Sir Paul McCartney.

Now well into his seventh decade, Bowie may no longer be a creative force in the music world, but few would still bet against him taking off on some new and interesting career tangent. (Just as long as he keeps that alto sax locked firmly in its case!)

Meanwhile, let's get back to those *Scary Monsters*…

IT'S NO GAME (PART 1)

It's best not to listen to this opening salvo while suffering from any kind of migraine or headache. Intense and angular, this is the musical equivalent of being trapped inside a meat grinder. In the movie *Falling Down*, Michael Douglas is driven mad by traffic jams, a nagging wife and a fly buzzing round his head. He was lucky he didn't play 'It's No Game (Part 1)' on his car radio or he might have gone ballistic much earlier in the movie.

The track begins with strange mechanical whirring and hissing sounds, which may be a vacuum cleaner or the studio coffee pot being pressed into action. Following the spoken count "1, 2, 2," (whatever happened to 3?), a Japanese lady begins her task of reciting Bowie's lyrics in the language of her forefathers. It's an intriguing dramatic device that works well, and indeed the sound of Michi Horita's voice, as she blazes out such phrases as "Shirnetto ya kage ga ka ku mei o miteiru", is more attractive than the composer's yells. It's fun to imagine what she might be singing about, but there is no need to speculate – Bowie obligingly translates by singing in English his tale of paranoia, claiming to be barred from the revolutionary main event. "I really don't understand the situation… people have their fingers broken. To be insulted by these fascists – it's so degrading." As he snarls out these angry statements, Fripp's guitar becomes out of kilter (a bit like the main theme in 'Park Life' by Blur). Soon the racket becomes too much even for Bowie, who positively bellows "Shut up!" in an attempt to bring the torture to an end. Indeed it is torture that Bowie protests about, the breaking of fingers in Chile, the plight of starving refugees seen nightly on TV news, and the violence on the streets.

The use of the Japanese voice is important to the song because, as Bowie said: "I wanted to break down a particular kind of sexist attitude about women and I thought that the Japanese girl typifies it. Everybody pictures a geisha girl as sweet, demure and non-thinking. So she sang the lyrics in a macho, Samurai voice.

UP THE HILL BACKWARDS

Released as the album's fourth single, it only reached Number 32 in the UK charts in April, 1981. The song deals with the problem of coping with the daily world situation, where horrors abound while we, the people, try to lead a normal life. So this is the essence of struggle – going up a hill backwards or, to put it another way, ascending an escalator on the London Underground that has been switched off for maintenance work.

It begins with acoustic guitars, played by Tony Visconti, and sets off at a moderate tempo with a Bo-Diddley-style rhythm. There are also overtones of The Who's 'Magic Bus'. A triangle makes a one-note appearance and Monkees-style backing vocals chirrup "It's got nothing to do with you" in support of Bowie's almost pleasant vocal.

But just to make sure no hint of superfluous jollity prevails, there is some more violent, off-the-wall lead guitar work. Bowie touches upon the impossibility of detaching the conscious self from the intrusions of the post-apocalyptic reality and revolutionary threat by singing "Yea yea yea – up the hill backwards, it'll be alright, ooo-ooo." That final "ooo-ooo" probably says more than all the Marxist Expressionism of Bertholt Brecht. The piece was originally going to be called 'Cameras In Brooklyn'.

SCARY MONSTER
(AND SUPER CREEPS)

One of the delights of living in a New York apartment is turning on the lights and finding cockroaches running all over the walls and ceilings. The same skittering effect is obtained here on this scampering plague of horrors. You want to turn an aerosol of Bug Blaster on to the guitarist as he runs up and down the scales, dropping notes in unexpected places. It's all part of the cunning artifice of the man – Bowie wants monsters, Fripp supplies them.

After another abrupt audible count, the rhythm is doubled up and Bowie begins to mutter in best Bewlay Brothers fashion.

Musically there is a strong industrial content to a piece that has all the rhythmic subtlety of an electric floor polisher. Bowie sings about a girl with blue eyes who could have been a killer and who opened strange doors that "we'd" never close again; she asked for his love and was given his "dangerous mind". It's hard not to surmise that he's talking about someone who once figured large in his life and had since gone. But the main talking point is not a stalking lover but that old she-devil, temptation.

This track was released as the third single from the album coupled with 'Because You're Young' and climbed into the UK Top 20 in January, 1981, but did little business in the USA.

ASHES TO ASHES

Undoubtedly the best song on the album and a deserved smash hit, it benefits from being built, mainly, around an appealing guitar synthesizer theme by Chuck Hammer. There is far less of the buzzing rock guitar that disrupts most of the other songs.

Interestingly, there are overtones of the Human League about 'Ashes', a tune that settles much more comfortably into the New Romantic and Techno Pop groove of the early Eighties. The Human League had begun life in 1977 by boldly announcing that conventional instruments were redundant; they concentrated on making music with synthesizers, sequencers and drum machines. In 1979, the band had supported Iggy Pop on his European tour and Bowie was intrigued. In December, 1981, Human League's 'Don't You Want Me' was Number 1 in the UK for five weeks and became the biggest UK single of the year, selling over a million copies and a further million in the US. 'Ashes To Ashes' shared some of that lustre.

Perhaps more significantly, it also brought back the subject of Major Tom, who first appeared on 'Space Oddity'. As Bowie looked back on his career he chortled: "We know Major Tom's a junkie", in other words something of a disappointment to those who thought of him as an archetypal all-British hero and the only true Englishman in space. The song describes his battle against drugs and seems to be a kind of penance: "I've never done good things, I've never done bad things, I've never done anything out of the blue."

This was Bowie's biggest hit in years and got to Number 1 in the UK charts, although it failed to crack the US market. The single version was backed with

'It's No Game' from *Lodger* and was accompanied by one of Bowie's most extraordinary videos, which is still played regularly on TV channels around the world. Directed by David Mallet, the video shows Bowie dressed as a sad clown with a white face and pointed hat. There are flashbacks to the astronaut of 'Space Oddity', and he is seen walking along a beach by a black sea, bathed in red light apparently in a funeral procession, being chased by a huge bulldozer and being harangued by his mother. It was one of the first great rock videos and set a trend for surrealism that became a staple diet of the genre.

FASHION

A bit of finger-wagging as Bowie warns the young of the dangers of following leaders, whether from the left or the right. A new dance craze or a political movement, it's all the same in the end. "Listen to me – don't listen to me, talk to me – don't talk to me," he says confusingly, but hoping those crazy kids get the message, somehow. "Ooop bop-do do do", he adds with the kind of lyrical intensity noted earlier in 'Up The Hill Backwards'. It's a pointed gibe at the disco culture but also a criticism of fascism, thus putting clear blue water between himself and two areas of which he clearly disapproved. Originally the song was based on a riff around the word "Jamaica" that could not be cajoled into a song structure until nearly the end of the recording session, when it became 'Fashion' and turned out to be another big hit, getting to Number 5 in the UK. The video was filmed in a dance studio and out on the streets of New York, featuring dancers, actors and models of all colours and creeds. Understandably, the song became very popular for use at fashion shows as the girls and boys start on the catwalks.

TEENAGE WILDLIFE

It's very long. Just when you think the band is going to stop they go on for another chorus. The tune is packed out with interminable guitar solos that could have been much better played by Mick Ronson. Or Bert Weedon. He could have done the whole session in a day. But this ambitious piece is where Judy Garland meets Shirley Bassey and Bowie goes into prima donna overdrive. It is also where a thirty-something man looks over his shoulder and suddenly realizes his rock 'n' roll teenage years have long since gone, despite every attempt to put off the inevitable. The opening few notes recall "Heroes" and it plods along with a drum beat that sounds like a man hammering a suitcase shut. The lyrics have an eerie kind of presentiment of impending doom about them – Bowie talks disparagingly about "One of the new wave boys, same old thing in brand new drag comes sweeping into view."

Bowie had an experience with a teenage millionaire who had taken him aside and begged for help saying: "David, what shall I do?" Some saw this as a reference to Gary Numan, who was pioneering his own brand of electro pop appeal at this time, and borrowing some of Bowie's fans in the process. In fact, it was a famous young American pop star of the Seventies who had hopped along to Bowie's doorstep one day and asked for advice on his future career moves. He probably wanted Bowie to write him a song. "They can't do this to me I'm not some piece of teenage wildlife," protests Bowie. He then goes on to sing: "Scream out aloud as they shoot you down" – an imaginary situation that hardly bears comment in view of subsequent events.

SCREAM LIKE A BABY

When Sid Vicious sang 'My Way' he developed a distinctly odd vocal style that may have been a subconscious influence on the lesser-known works of Bowie. This is undoubtedly one of his lesser-known works – and deservedly so. Stylistically speaking, it has the kind of trampolining rhythm and hurdy gurdy keyboard effect that made 'Have I The Right' by the Honeycombs such a big hit in 1964. Honey Lantree meets Sid Vicious. But this melting pot of styles and cultural referencing all contributes to the canon of Bowie's work, as any good style-guru or fashion-fascist will tell you. It certainly confuses the humble listener, who may well come away from 'Scream Like A Baby' scratching his head in dismay.

The tune has its origins in a 1973 piece written for Ava Cherry's group The Astronettes called 'I Am A Laser'. It is a piece of science fiction about the adventures of his friend Sam, who gets beaten up in the street (presumably by a Goon Squad coming to town – beep, beep). "They came down hard on the faggots!" yells Bowie at one point. Sam is thrown into a wagon blindfolded, chained, and stomped on. He swears revenge and screams like a baby as he refuses to be cowed into becoming a part of a society that he rejects. Sadly he is fated to meet a ghastly end before he and Bowie can have the fun together they never knew.

On a more serious level this is a song about racial prejudice and police repression and the victimization that greets all who dare to be different. But it all becomes too overblown. Bowie makes interesting use of vari-speed vocals to emphasize the air of schizophrenia in the last few moments of the song. Split music for a split personality. 'Scream Like A Baby' was coupled with 'Fashion' for single release.

KINGDOM COME

This is that rare Bowie event, a cover song – in this case, written by Tom Verlaine, formerly of the band Television. The song harks back to the kind of post-punk New York rock that perhaps Bowie found more attractive than contemporary English techno pop.

But of course there is always a danger of reading too much into influences and the conflicting attractions of different strands of pop-music culture. Bowie might simply have been dictated to by the mood of the day, what he'd read in the newspapers that morning and how many cigarettes he smoked before breakfast. In this case it was Carlos Alomar who suggested doing the song, which David sings with all available power and conviction.

BECAUSE YOU'RE YOUNG

One of the reasons performances like this lack any kind of real strength or direction is that they are bereft of the type of musical expression that should be contributed by the backing musicians. They are there as functionaries. Although Fripp makes plenty of scary noises on his tracks, there is little sense of a band creating meaningful music together. The drums and bass are a case in point. They plod away as part of a rhythm track that sounds like it was put down when the rest of the band members were off shopping or playing golf. From the excessive soloing and loose interaction of the early Seventies, the production process had seen a radical shift in the opposite direction, resulting in the anonymous thud of a drummer locked in a sound booth, and sheets of synthesizer that are closer to the cacophony of a fairground than the sound of collective improvisation. In the right circumstances, a traditional band performance can inspire a singer to greater heights.

On the bright side, 'Because You're Young' and other tracks on *Scary Monsters* marked a shift back to more audience-friendly work. At least Bowie was playing in a recognizable pop format again. But, compared to the flashes sparked by 'Fashion' and 'Ashes', this item was not particularly inspirational.

Pete Townshend plays guitar but doesn't make any noticeable impact – although, according to Bowie, he jumped around and did some Who-style arm 'windmilling' during the recording. The piece proffers advice to his son Joe and has some thoughts on the recent break-up of his marriage as well as on what the future might hold. It's deeply personal – indulging in debates about the lyrics is less important than respecting the feelings of the composer. Bowie says it all when he sings: "She took back everything she said, left him nearly out of his mind", so he'll just dance his life away with a million dreams and a million scars.

IT'S NO GAME (PART 2)

The CD reissue of *Scary Monsters* contained the bonus tracks 'Space Oddity' (acoustic version), a re-recording of 'Panic In Detroit' from the 'Aladdin Sane' period, 'Crystal Japan' recorded for a Japanese Saki TV advertisement and 'Alabama Song', a studio version of a Kurt Weill/Bertholt Brecht song, which was released as a single in 1980 and got to Number 23 in the UK chart.

The vinyl version of the album concludes with a reprise of the opening number. The Japanese singer has now disappeared and Bowie gives one of his finest vocal performances on the album – and perhaps in some years. He's calmed down, sings with great assurance and sounds like he means every word. Even when he repeats the phrase about being "insulted by these fascists" he sounds resigned, mature and in control of himself. The monster has been tamed and put to rest.

The strangest things still happen on Bowie albums however. The song contains the line "Put a bullet in my brain and it makes all the papers... it's no game." It certainly wasn't. Two references to shootings on one album seemed more like a premonition than a coincidence. In December, 1980, Radio 1 DJ Andy Peebles went to interview Bowie in New York about *Scary Monsters* and his role in *The Elephant Man*. By chance, Andy also met John Lennon, who was in town, and talked to him about his touring plans. Two days later Lennon was shot dead.

Bowie disappeared from the music scene for two years after the tragedy of John Lennon's murder, and refused to promote *Scary Monsters* with any live shows. When he returned in 1983, it was to perform less controversial material. The days of being the wild-eyed boy from outer space were over. From now on, pop's favourite changeling would remain just David Bowie – the superstar for all seasons.

CHRONOLOGY 1947–1980

January 8, 1947
David Robert Jones born at 40 Stansfield Road, Brixton, London.

1955
David, aged eight, moves with half brother Terry Burns to live with an uncle in Yorkshire.

1957
David and Terry return to South East London to live with their parents Heywood and Margaret Jones in Plaistow Grove, Bromley.

September, 1958
David attends Bromley Technical High School.

March, 1961
David's left eye damaged in a school fight over a girl. As a result he has different coloured eyes.

July, 1962
The Kon-Rads formed, featuring Dave Jay (David Jones) and friend George Underwood. The group are turned down by Decca and break up.

December, 1962
David plays the saxophone with George and The Dragons at end of term show at Bromley Technical High School. He shares the bill with The Little Ravens, featuring 12-year-old Peter Frampton on guitar.

July, 1963
David leaves school and starts work at an advertising agency.

December, 1963
David joins Bromley R&B group, The King Bees. David writes to washing machine tycoon John Bloom for help – he refers him to agent Les

Conn, who signs the group.

June 5,1964
The King Bees are signed to Vocation, a subsidiary of Decca. David Jones and The King Bees release their first single, 'Liza Jane'/'Louie Louie Go Home'.

September, 1964
The King Bees release a second flop single 'You're Holding Me Down'/'I've Gotta' (Coral). The singer now refers to himself as Davy Jones and joins a second group, The Manish Boys. The King Bees split.

December, 1964
The Manish Boys tour with Gene Pitney, The Kinks and Marianne Faithfull

February, 1965
David Jones turns down booking on the BBC TV show *Gadzooks! It's All Happening* when they demand he cut his long hair

March 5, 1965
David Jones and The Manish Boys release 'I Pity The Fool'/'Take My Tip' (Parlophone), produced by Shel Talmy. 'Take My Tip' is David's first original song on record. Sessionman Jimmy Page plays lead guitar.

August 20, 1965
David Jones releases single 'You've Got A Habit Of Leaving'/'Baby Loves It That Way'. He meets pop manager Ken Pitt, who grooms him for stardom and takes him away from Parlophone to sign to Pye.

January 14, 1966
Davy Jones changes his name

to David Bowie to avoid confusion with Davy Jones of The Monkees. He releases 'Can't Help Thinking About Me'/ 'And I Say To Myself (Pye) as David Bowie and The Lower Third.

February 7, 1966
Bowie forms new group The Buzz and plays The Marquee, London on February 11.

April 1, 1966
First solo single under Bowie's own name 'Do Anything You Say'/ 'Goodmorning Girl'

November 8, 1966
Ken Pitt goes to New York and meets Andy Warhol and Lou Reed, and brings Bowie back influential Velvet Underground album

December 2, 1966
David Bowie solo single 'Rubber Band'/'The London Boys' (Deram) released.

April 14, 1967
'The Laughing Gnome'/ 'The Gospel According To Tony Day' released. Reissued in 1973, it gets to Number 4 in the charts.

April 25, 1967
Bowie signs management contract with Ken Pitt.

June 1, 1967
Debut *David Bowie* album featuring 'Love You Till Tuesday', released on Deram and later reissued as *The World Of David Bowie*.

December 18, 1967
Appearance on BBC's TV's *Top Gear*.

December 28, 1967
Bowie makes his debut as a

mime artist with Lindsay Kemp in *Pierrot In Turquoise* at the New Theatre, Oxford.

January 30, 1968
Bowie dances a minuet with girlfriend Hermione Farthingale in BBC 2 TV drama *The Pistol Shot*.

March 5, 1968
Mime performance in *Pierrot In Turquoise* at the Mercury Theatre in Notting Hill Gate, London.

June 3, 1968
Bowie performs both mime and songs at the Royal Festival Hall, London supporting Marc Bolan's Tyrannosaurus Rex.

September, 1968
Inspired by Stanley Kubrick's *2001: A Space Odyssey* movie, Bowie writes hit song 'Space Oddity'

February 22, 1969
Bowie supports Marc Bolan's Tyrannosaurus Rex UK tour with a mime show.

April 9, 1969
Bowie meets Mary Angela Barnett at the Speakeasy Club, Margaret Street, London at a King Crimson press reception.

June 20, 1969
Bowie signs to Mercury Records, having recorded 'Space Oddity'.

July 11, 1969
'Space Oddity' released and becomes a Number 5 hit in the UK charts in November.

August 5, 1969
Heywood Stenton Jones, Bowie's father, dies of pneumonia.

August 16, 1969
Bowie organizes festival in Beckenham Park, inspiring the song 'Memory Of A Free Festival'.

October 8, 1969
Bowie supports Humble Pie on UK tour and his acoustic set is booed by Pie fans.

November 4, 1969
Second album *David Bowie* (Philips) released.

February 22, 1970
Bowie's new band The Hype make debut at The Roundhouse, Chalk Farm with Mick Ronson on guitar.

March 6, 1970
Marc Bolan plays lead guitar on latest Bowie single release 'The Prettiest Star'

March 20, 1970
Bowie marries Angela Barnett at Bromley Registry Office.

May, 1970
Tony Defries takes over management from Ken Pitt.

January 27, 1971
Bowie visits America to promote *The Man Who Sold The World* and meets Andy Warhol and Lou Reed in New York.

April, 1971
The Man Who Sold The World (Mercury). album released in the UK. The cover shows him wearing a dress, which receives a hostile reaction in America.

May 28, 1971
David and Angela's son Duncan Zowie Haywood Jones Bowie is born.

September, 1971
Bowie signs to RCA Records during a business visit to New York with his manager.

December 17, 1971
Bowie's fourth album *Hunky Dory* (RCA) is released.

January 22, 1972
Melody Maker interview in which Bowie proclaims 'I'm gay and always have been'. The resultant publicity helps make him a superstar.

February 3, 1972
Bowie starts a seven-month UK tour during which 'Ziggy Stardust' character evolves.

June 9, 1972
The Rise And Fall OfZiggy Stardust And The Spiders From Mars (RCA) released.

September 1972
First major US tour starts to rave notices from the critics.

September 1, 1972
New single 'John I'm Only Dancing'/'Hang On To Yourself' (RCA) released.

November, 1972
'The Jean Genie'/'Ziggy Stardust' (RA) single is released.

February 14, 1973
Bowie begins world tour in New York. Mike Garson joins Bowie on piano.

April 13, 1973
Aladdin Sane (RCA) is fastest selling album since Beatles heyday with 100,000 advance orders.

May 12, 1973
Bowie starts a British tour at Earls Court, in London.

June 22, 1973
'Life On Mars'/The Man Who Sold The World' (RCA) single released.

July 3, 1973
Shock retirement of Ziggy Stardust announced at end of Odeon Hammersmith concert. Says Bowie: "This is the last show we'll ever do." It isn't.

October, 1973
Bowie releases *Pin Ups* (RCA) album of cover versions of favourite R&B and pop hits as an antidote to 'Ziggy'.

February 15, 1974
'Rebel Rebel'/'Queen Bitch' (RCA), Bowie's seventeenth single, released.

April, 1974
Diamond Dogs (RCA) album released.

June 14, 1974
Bowie's longest North American tour opens in Montreal, with Bowie backed by a new band to replace the Spiders From Mars.

October, 1974
David Live (RCA) double live album is released, culled from performances made on July 14 and 15, 1974 at the Tower Theatre, Philadelphia.

March, 1975
Young Americans (RCA) album released. Bowie takes up residence in Los Angeles and appears in the feature film *The Man Who Fell To Earth*.

May, 1975
Images (Deram), a compilation of his mid-Sixties work, is released.

August, 1975
'Fame'/'Right' (RCA) single culled from the *Young Americans* album. 'Fame', with backing vocals from John Lennon, becomes David Bowie's first Number One hit in the US.

September 26, 1975
Reissued 'Space Oddity' is David Bowie's first Number One British chart hit.

January 23, 1976
Station To Station (RCA) album is released.

May 3, 1976
First of six nights of concerts at London's Wembley Arena.

January 8, 1977
David Bowie celebrates his thirtieth birthday in Berlin, followed by release of *Low* (RCA) album on January 14.

September 9, 1977
Bowie guests on Marc Bolan's *Marc Show* in Manchester.

September 16, 1977
Bowie's friend Marc Bolan is killed in a car crash on Barnes Common in London. Bowie attends funeral.

October, 1977
"Heroes" (RCA) album released, hailed as a classic after 'difficult' *Low*.

September 25, 1978
Stage (RCA) double live album is released with Adrian Belew and Carlos Alomar on guitars.

May 25, 1979
Lodger (RCA), Bowie's sixteenth album, is released.

August, 1980
'Ashes To Ashes'/'Move On' single released and tops UK charts.

September 12, 1980
Release of *Scary Monsters (And Supercreeps)*, Bowie's last album for RCA.

DISCOGRAPHY: SINGLES 1964–1980

DAVIE JONES AND THE KING
BEES
Liza Jane/Louie Louie Go Home
(Vocalion POP V 9221)
(May 1964)

THE MANISH BOYS
I Pity the Fool/Take My Tip
(Parlophone R 5250)
(March 1965)

DAVY JONES AND THE
LOWER THIRD
You've Got A Habit Of Leaving/
Baby Loves That Way
(Parlophone R 5315)
(August 1965)

DAVID BOWIE AND THE
LOWER THIRD
Can't Help Thinking About Me/
And I Say To Myself
(Pye 7N 17020) **(January 1966)**

DAVID BOWIE
Do Anything You Say/Good
Morning Girl (Pye 7N 17079)
(April 1966)

I Dig Everything/I'm Not Losing
Sleep (Pye 7N 17157)
(August 1966)

Rubber Band/The London Boys
(Deram DM 107)
(December 1966)

The Laughing Gnome/The
Gospel According To Tony Day
(Deram DM123) **(April 1967)**

Love You Till Tuesday/Did You
Ever Have A Dream
(Deram DM 135) **(July 1967)**

Space Oddity/Wild-Eyed Boy
From Free Cloud
(Philips BF 1801) **(July 1969)**

The Prettiest Star/Conversation
Piece (Mercury MF 1135)
(March 1970)

Memory Of A Free Festival (Part

1)/(Part 2) (Mercury 6052 026)
(June 1970)

Holy Holy/Black Country Rock
(Mercury 6052 049)
(January 1971)

Changes/Andy Warhol
(RCA 2160) **(February 1972)**

Starman/Suffragette City
(RCA 2199) **(April 1972)**

John, I'm Only Dancing/Hang
Onto Yourself (RCA 2263)
(September 1972)

Do Anything You Say/I Dig
Everything/I Can't Help Thinking
About Me/I'm Not Losing Sleep
(Pye 7NX 8002)
(October 1972)

The Jean Genie/Ziggy Stardust
(RCA 2302) **(November 1972)**

Drive-In Saturday/Round And
Round (RCA 2352)
(April 1973)

John, I'm Only Dancing
(alternate version)/Hang Onto
Yourself (RCA 2263)
(April 1973)

Life On Mars/The Man Who
Sold The World (RCA 2316)
(June 1973)

The Laughing Gnome/The
Gospel According To Tony Day
(Deram DM 123)
(September 1973)

Sorrow/Amsterdam (RCA 2424)
(October 1973)

Rebel Rebel/Lady Grinning Soul
(RCA APBO 0287)
(February 1974)

Rock'n'Roll Suicide/Quicksand
(RCA LPBO 5021) **(April 1974)**

Diamond Dogs/Holy Holy
(RCA APBO 0293)
(June 1974)

Knock On Wood (live)/Panic In
Detroit (live) (RCA 2466)
(September 1974)

Young Americans/Suffragette
City (RCA 2523)
(February 1975)

The London Boys/Love You Till
Tuesday (Decca F 13579)
(May 1975)

Fame/Right (RCA 2579)
(July 1975)

Space Oddity/Changes/Velvet
Goldmine (RCA 2593)
(September 1975)

Golden Years/Can You Hear Me
(RCA 2640) **(November 1975)**

TVC-15/We Are The Dead
(RCA 2682) **(April 1976)**

Suffragette City/Stay
(RCA 2726) **(July 1976)**

Sound And Vision/A New
Career In A New Town
(RCA PB 0905) **(January 1977)**

Be My Wife/Speed Of Life (RCA
PB 1017) **(June 1977)**

Heroes/V-2 Schneider
(RCAPB 1121)
(September 1977)

Beauty And The Beast/Sense Of
Doubt (RCAPB 1190)
(January 1978)

Liza Jane /Louie Louie Come
Home (Decca F 13807)
(September 1978)

The Laughing Gnome/The
Gospel According To Tony (Day
Deram DM 123)

(September 1978)

Breaking Glass (live)/Ziggy
Stardust (live)/Art Decade (live)
(RCA BOW 1) **(October 1978)**

I Pity The Fool/Take My Tip/
You've Got A Habit Of
Leaving/ Baby Loves That Way
(EMI 2925) **(March 1979)**

Boys Keep Swinging/Fantastic
Voyage (RCA BOW 2)
(April 1979)

DJ/Repetition (RCA BOW 2)
(September 1979)

John, I'm Only Dancing (Again)
(1975) /John, I'm Only Dancing
(1972) (RCA BOW 4)
(December 1979)

John, I'm Only Dancing
(Again) (1975) (Extended)/John,
I'm Only Dancing (1972)
(12-inch) (RCA BOW 12-4)
(December 1979)

Alabama Song/Space Oddity
(RCA BOW 5) **(February 1980)**

Ashes to Ashes/Move On
(RCA BOW 6) **(August 1980)**

Fashion/Scream Like A Baby
(RCA BOW 7) **(October 1980)**

Fashion/Scream Like A Baby (12
inch) (RCA BOWT 7)
(October 1980)

Scary Monsters (And Super
Creeps)/Because You're Young
(RCA BOW 8) **(January 1981)**

DISCOGRAPHY: ALBUMS 1967–1980

June 2, 1967
David Bowie
Uncle Arthur; Sell Me A Coat; Rubber Band; Love You Till Tuesday; There Is A Happy Land; We Are Hungry Men; When I Live My Dream; Little Bombardier; Silly Boy Blue; Come And Buy My Toys; Join the Gang; She's Got Medals; Maids Of Bond Street; Please Mr Gravedigger Deram DML 1007 (mono) Deram SML 1007 (stereo) Deram 18003 (US) (excluding We Are Hungry Men, Maids Of Bond Street)

November 4, 1969
David Bowie
Space Oddity; Unwashed And Somewhat Slightly Dazed; Letter To Hermione; Cygnet Committee; Janine; An Occasional Dream; Wild Eyed Boy From Freecloud; God Knows I'm Good; Memory Of A Free Festival Philips SBL 7912. Released 'Man Of Words, Man Of Music' (US)

March 1970
The World Of David Bowie
Uncle Arthur; Love You Till Tuesday; There Is A Happy Land; Little Bombardier; Sell Me A Coat; Silly Boy Blue; The London Boys; Karma Man; Rubber Band; Let Me Sleep Beside You; Come And Buy My Toys; She's Got Medals; In The Heat Of The Morning; When I Live My Dream

April 1971
The Man Who Sold The World
The Width Of A Circle; All the Madmen; Black Country Rock; After All; Running Gun Blues; Saviour Machine; She Shook Me Cold; The Man Who Sold The World; The Supermen

December 17, 1971
Hunky Dory
Changes; Oh! You Pretty Things; Eight Line Poem; Life On Mars?; Kooks; Quicksand; Fill Your Heart; Andy Warhol; Song For Bob Dylan; Queen Bitch; The Bewlay Brothers

June 6, 1972
The Rise And Fall Of Ziggy Stardust And The Spiders From Mars
Five Years; Soul Love; Moonage Daydream; Starman; It Ain't Easy; Lady Stardust; Star; Hang On To Yourself; Ziggy Stardust; Suffragette City; Rock V Roll Suicide

April 13, 1973
Aladdin Sane
Watch That Man; Aladdin Sane; Drive-in Saturday; Panic In Detroit; Cracked Actor; Time; The Prettiest Star; Let's Spend The Night Together; The Jean Genie; Lady Grinning Soul

October 19, 1973
Pin-Ups
Rosalyn; Here Comes The Night; I Wish You Would; See Emily Play; Everything's Alright; I Can't Explain; Friday On My Mind; Sorrow; Don't Bring Me Down; Shapes Of Things; Anyway, Anyhow, Anywhere; Where Have All The Good Times Gone

April 24, 1974
Diamond Dogs
Future Legend; Diamond Dogs; Sweet Thing; Candidate; Sweet Thing (reprise); Rebel Rebel; Rock 'n' Roll With Me; We Are The Dead; 1984; Big Brother; Chant Of The Ever Circling Skeletal Family

October 29, 1974
David Live
1984; Rebel Rebel; Moonage Daydream; Sweet Thing; Changes; Suffragette City; Aladdin Sane; All The Young Dudes; Cracked Actor; Rock 'n' Roll With Me; Watch That Man; Knock On Wood; Diamond Dogs; Big Brother; Width Of A Circle; The Jean Genie; Rock 'n' Roll Suicide

March 7, 1975
Young Americans
Young Americans; Win; Fascination; Right; Somebody Up There Likes Me; Across The Universe; Can You Hear Me; Fame

May, 1975
Images 1966-67
Rubber Band; Maids of Bond Street; Sell Me A Coat; Love Gnome; The Gospel According To Tony Day; Did You Ever Have A Dream; Uncle Arther; We Are Hungry Men; When I Live My Dream; Join The Gang; Little Bombardier; Come And Buy My Toys; Silly Boy Blue; She's Got Medals; Please Mr Gravedigger; London Boys; Karma Man; Let Me Sleep Beside You; In The Heat Of The Morning Deram DPA 3017/3018 Join The Gang; Little Bombardier; Come And Buy My Toys; Silly Boy Blue; She's Got Medals; Please Mr Gravedigger; London Boys; Karma Man; Let Me Sleep Beside You; In The Heat Of The Morning Deram

January 23, 1976
Station To Station
Station To Station; Golden Years; Word On A Wing; TVC15; Stay; Wild Is The Wind

May 1976
Changesonebowie
Space Oddity; John I'm Only Dancing; Changes; Ziggy Stardust; Suffragette City; The Jean Genie; Diamond Dogs; Rebel Rebel; Young Americans; Fame; Golden Years

January 14, 1977
Low
Speed Of Life; Breaking Glass; What In The World; Sound And Vision; Always Crashing In The Same Car; Be My Wife; A New Career In A New Town; Warszawa; Art Decade; Weeping Wall; Subterraneans

October 14, 1977
"Heroes"
Beauty And The Beast; Joe The Lion; ""Heroes""; Sons Of The Silent Age; Blackout; V-2 Schneider; Sense Of Doubt; Moss Garden; Neukoln; The Secret Life Of Arabia

September 25, 1978
Stage
Hang On To Yourself; Ziggy Stardust; Five Years; Soul Love; Star; Station To Station; Fame; TVC 15; Warszawa; Speed Of Life; Art Decade; Sense Of Doubt; Breaking Glass; "Heroes"; What In The World; Blackout; Beauty And The Beast

May 18, 1979
Lodger
Fantastic Voyage; African Night Flight; Move On; Yassassin; Red Sails; DJ; Look Back In Anger; Boys Keep Swinging; Repetition; Red Money; I Pray; Ole; Look Back In Anger

September 12, 1980
Scary Monsters (And Supercreeps)
It's No Game (Part 1); Up The Hill Backwards; Scary Monsters (And Supercreeps); Ashes To Ashes; Fashion; Teenage Wildlife; Scream Like A Baby; Kingdom Come; Because You're Young; It's No Game (Part 2)

189

INDEX